The Hidden Story
of the
Kilsyth Weavers

TOM CRAINEY

ARGYLL ✢ PUBLISHING

Argyll Publishing
Glendaruel
Argyll PA22 3AE
Scotland
www.argyllpublishing.co.uk

British Library Cataloguing-in-Publication Data.
A catalogue record for this book is available from the British Library.

ISBN 978 1 908931 30 6

Printing & Binding PB Print UK

dedicated to the cherished memory
of
John Patrick of Allanfauld

The Weaver – painting by Leon Augustin Lhermitte – Glasgow Museum Collection

Acknowledgments

I am deeply grateful to the following for their generous assistance, support, corrections and advice in the production of this narrative.

The Coal Industry Special Welfare Fund for a contribution towards the cost of publishing;
John Cullen, Tommy Canavan and Jim Abercrombie;
The Rev. Alastair McLachlan;
Craig Wishart, Session Clerk Eaglesham Parish Church;
Don Martin, the doyen of Scottish Local History;
John Gordon with his encyclopaedic knowledge of the history of Kilsyth;
Willie Chalmers, who has made an immense contribution in recording and preserving Kilsyth's history;
Croy Historical Society;
Mrs. Jane Lauder and her excellent staff at Kilsyth Library;
David Smith of the William Patrick Library, Kirkintilloch;
staff at the libraries of Glasgow and Strathclyde Universities and the National Archives of Scotland;
staff at the Mitchell Library Glasgow;
staff at the Summerlee Museum of Scottish Industrial Life, Coatbridge;
David Forsyth of the National Museum of Scotland;
Tom Kinvig and Archie Waddell of the Kilsyth Anderson Church;
Bill Gracie, author of 'Kilsyth Burns' Old Parish Church.

I, of course, accept the entire responsibility for the content and any errors that may have occurred.

Tom Crainey

Contents

FOREWORD

AS A KILSYTH schoolboy, and not a particularly studious one at that, one question intrigued me: what was the story of the Kilsyth weavers? We knew that in the age before Kilsyth became a coal mining town most Kilsythians were handloom weavers, operating their own businesses from their own cottages. They were visibly represented in the Burgh's coat of arms by the shuttle, but beyond that – nothing.

The conservative-inclined former parish minister, the Rev. Peter Anton, even succeeded in writing a history of the parish with barely a passing reference to the weavers, although, as we shall find, their lives and times were more significant, interesting and relevant than many of the rich and ennobled who were featured. For those who had access to a copy some of the gaps were filled in by the Rev. Robert Anderson in his commendable *A History of Kilsyth* and a *Memorial of Two Lives*.

It did not require extensive research, however, to discover that the exclusion of the weavers from our history was no accident. We were encouraged to rejoice in the fact that we were all sons and daughters of the British Empire blessed to live in a democracy which is the guarantor of our rights, liberties and citizenship. The unspoken impression was that these rights were a gift from a united nation.

The truth is somewhat different. Every small step towards creating our democracy was cruelly resisted and heroically won by ordinary men and women who were called upon to pay a heavy price. In the vanguard of that great cause were the Scottish handloom weavers who were recognised as the best educated working class in Europe. But what came as a revelation was that the Kilsyth weavers, whose descendants walk the streets of Kilsyth today, not only played a part in that epic struggle, but a highly significant part. It is remarkable that the Parish of Kilsyth, which covered an area of seven miles by four and with a population in 1801 of only 1,762 should have been recognised by friend and foe alike as one of the principal centres in the battle for democracy.

This narrative, however, does not look into the lives of those Kilsyth weavers like some isolated historical curiosity. Rather, we emulate those weavers themselves who looked outwards to the values, personalities and issues which shaped their lives and the world they lived in, and moved them to resolve to make the world anew. I found their story instructive and inspiring. You will form your own judgment.

Tom Crainey
January 2013

The Rev. John Anderson 'Kilsyth minister, Scholar, Democrat and friend of Thomas Muir'

CHAPTER 1

IT KICKED OFF sometime around the 1750s and lasted 150 dramatic and tumultuous years. As late as the early1900s there remained one solitary Kilsyth handloom weaver still at work in his loomshop, a relic to a vanished past.

But we can capture something of the flavour of the Kilsyth weaver's life from those who lived at the time, or near enough to know. Writing in 1893 a local author recalled the scene and circumstances of the weavers some years earlier.

> 'As the mining industry had not in those days assumed by any means the importance it occupies in the Burgh today, and as the shuttle still fitted to and fro on the 'lags' of nearly 1,000 looms in Kilsyth the majority (of a party of merrymakers she was writing about) were weavers, or of that fraternity.'

> 'Being in a manner their own masters as regards time, they took a holiday when so inclined, and as, with the exception of the period which embraced the American Civil War (1861/65) which almost completely cut off the supply of cotton, wages were fairly remunerative, and food was plain and cheap. They were on the whole a contented and happy class. If a knight of the shuttle could boast of a pair of white moleskin trousers and thick tweed coat, and his wife a plain wincey gown and Paisley plaid for attending the Kirk, they were considered fairly well off and bien. If a newly married pair could start home free of debt with a chair or two, a table, a bed, a few pots and pans and a modest assortment of napery, all contained in a single apartment, their so-called poverty gave them little trouble.

'Either one could earn the bread of the family at the loom, and as long as work was plentiful, want did not appear prominently as one of the afflictions of their existence. We need make no comment here on the many changes which the passing years have brought about in these and in other matters as they must be apparent to everyone who remembers the conditions which existed auld lang syne.' (1)

The Rev. Robert Anderson, who was born and raised in Kilsyth and went on to succeed his father as the weavers' minister in the Relief Church, knew as much as anyone about the life, character and qualities of the weaver in the 1800s. He remembered them as:

'a kindly social race. This spirit did not prevail much between the rival camps of the Auld Kirk and the Relief, into which the community was divided, still it pulsed behind the barriers, not infrequently broke through them, and ruled in both camps. The weavers were intelligent as well as kindly. They liked solid reading. It was not with them the halfpenny newspaper and the illustrated monthly. In those old days bound books of religion, history, poetry, and philosophy lay on the drawers head and on the window sill, as well as on the weaver's loom as he drove the shuttle. In addition to their own, my father's books were often in their houses, Rollin's *Ancient History*, Gibbon's *Decline and Fall of the Roman Empire*, Hume's *History of England*, etc. The weavers were an independent class of people. They did not know what it was to 'snool' to any man. They did not need. They were their own masters and feu-owners of their own thatched homesteads, and with anything like fair trade could regulate their own work and winnings. Their comfortable dwellings usually consisted of a well furnished room and plenished kitchen, with perhaps a garret, reached by a stair door in the kitchen corner. The loomshops, of four, six or eight looms, as the case might be, was across the trance or lobby, which led from the front door to the back garden, with its apple and cherry trees, its potato and cabbage plots, the seed beds and borders of old fashioned flowers. It must have been a treat to my father, and, at the beginning of my ministry, more than fifty years ago, I was not without it myself, when sitting talking with the gudeman at the kitchen fire, to hear, when the loomshop door was opened, the full-throated rendering of some auld Scotch sang, rising high and sweet above the sound of lay and shuttle. When trade was good, the weavers were well off. Their food was simple, but substantial and abundant. Loaf bread was little used. There were 'luggies' in the morning, filled with porridge 'chief of Scotia's food'. The well trampled oatmeal supplied the meal both for the porridge and the crisp oatmeal cakes. There was always plenty of buttermilk, bought from the farmers' carts. There were cheeses and crocks of salted butter stowed away. The 'girdle' was often on the fire for cakes and scones of various sorts – flour scones, barleymeal scones and potato scones. There was usually a jar of peasemeal, not only for 'brose' when wanted, but to mix with buttermilk as a favourite summer drink.' (2)

These reflections were no doubt true but they were far from being the whole truth. It will be noted that both accounts qualify the somewhat idyllic picture of the weaver's life. The first writer states 'as long as work was plentiful, want did not appear prominently as one of the afflictions of their existence'. Anderson states that 'with anything like fair trade they could regulate their own work and winnings,' and adds 'when trade was good, the weavers were well off.'

But the fact is that often trade was not good and work was not plentiful. Even during the Golden Age which lasted from the infancy of the industry until the great strike of 1812 there were four major recessions and many other slumps in a trade which was notoriously volatile. The margin between prosperity and destitution was narrow, with hardship only a fall-off in trade away. Should that coincide with a bad harvest the spectre of hardship and starvation loomed. They took whatever measures they could to protect themselves against the bad times, such as taking a drill in local farmers' fields to grow their own vegetables, the pay-off being that they returned to their rural roots at harvest time to help the farmers. They also cultivated vegetables in long stretches of gardens, which are still discernable at Shuttle Street where the gardens ran from the rear of their cottages down to the Hedges and Dykes footpath.

When the industry was still in its infancy, the Kilsyth Society of Weavers was set up in 1760 to provide a measure of protection during the hard times. The membership grew steadily and by 1795 had 350 members. A new member paid 7/6 up-front and one shilling yearly. If confined to bed through illness a member received three shillings weekly; strangely, if only unable to work, but walking about, a member received an additional two shillings. When a member died his family were awarded £2 sterling to meet funeral expenses. Through prudent investment the fund grew to £300; this was partly due to the fact that the weaver had 'an honest pride in supporting himself and his family, and a great aversion to come upon the funds unless forced to do so.' (3)

Neither could their daily routine be regarded as leisurely. Even during the 'Golden Age' the working day was long:

> 'The day began with the public crier walking the streets beating his drum at 5am. The hour for beginning work was six o'clock, and the men might have another snooze, but their wives or daughters had to rise and break-up the 'gathering coal' and not only that, but get as many 'pirns' filled as would keep the looms going from six o'clock till breakfast time at nine. The dinner was at two o'clock, and supper at six. The day's task, as a rule, was over at eight in the evening.' (4)

Nevertheless, the change in their lives and prospects was more dramatic than any we have known in modern times or could imagine. Until then, day-to-day life had gone on in the same fashion for centuries. Kilsyth was little more than a hamlet with most people living and scraping an existence in or around pre-capitalist farms scattered around the Parish of Kilsyth, bordered by the Carron River in the North and the Kelvin River in the south, and running from the

Bushburn this side of Banknock in the East to the Woodburn west of Queenzieburn.

The peasants had virtually no legal or human rights. They existed almost totally at the mercy of the aristocratic landowners and their baron courts, and there was little mercy on offer. Any dissent was ruthlessly crushed and the nobility were in a position to sanitise or destroy the records to escape the verdict of history. They did not, however, completely succeed.

Thomas Carlyle in the eighteenth century delivered this scathing judgment:

> 'It is noteworthy that the nobles of Scotland have maintained a
> quite despicable behaviour from the days of Wallace downwards
> – a selfish, ferocious, famishing, unprincipled set of hyenas,
> from whom at no time, and in no way, has this country derived
> any benefit whatever.'

Tom Johnston, who later was to represent Kilsyth in Parliament, and who is widely regarded as the greatest Scottish Secretary of the twentieth century, expanded on that indictment.

> 'Generation after generation, these few families of tax gatherers
> have sucked the life-blood of our nation; in their prides and
> lusts they have sent us to war, family against family, clan against
> clan, race against race. That they might live in idleness and
> luxury, the labouring man has sweated and starved; they have
> pruned the creeds of our church and stolen its revenues. . . In
> the age before the Reformation we found the nobles who had
> allied themselves to our cause, not only foisting a hateful
> patronage upon our pulpits, but burning the ancient charters,
> grabbing the lands, and despoiling the patrimony of the kirk.
> They scorned every principle of morality we hold dear, they
> gambled and murdered and robbed. . . they destroyed our
> ancient freedom, corrupted our laws, despoiled us of our
> common heritage, the soil, and today take rents for which they
> cannot produce titles.' (5)

Against this national background, and denied any democratic rights, the peasants could have had little time to spare from the task of keeping body and soul together. On top of the social control, there was the ingrained feudal culture that held you were what you were born. Any aspirations to control or change your life was unthinkable. To be delivered from this servitude, and within a few years to become the 'aristocrats of labour' with their skills in demand and attracting a living wage along with the degree of independence that went with it was deliverance beyond the dreams of those early weavers.

There is reason to believe that Kilsyth was ahead of most of the west of Scotland communities in embracing the new handloom weaving industry. Prior to the take-off there had been 'country weavers' at work for centuries, and Kilsyth's involvement in that early cottage industry probably provided a head start. In those pre-industrial days local farmers grew and harvested flax. This was then processed at the Burngreen, which had been a public park going back for centuries to the days of the Livingstones. The flax was 'retted' – that is placed in the Garrell Burn to remove the woody external covering of the fibres by rotting. This operation would be completed by beating out the unwanted material.

Robert Anderson remembered as a boy seeing the old 'beetlin stane' at the head of the Burngreen where in the past the flax was 'beetl'it.' This process was later carried out in lint mills. According to tradition one existed at the north east corner of the Inns Park. There was another on the banks of the Garrell and one situated close to the present Croy railway station. However, after the flax was 'retted', the fibres were combed into strands which could then be spun – it was then that the material was called linen.

After weaving, the linen was laid out on the Burngreen for the lengthy process of bleaching. The spinning operation was carried out by girls and women, supplying work for unmarried women, thus the term spinster. Women could also considerably boost the family income by tambouring, or embroidery. Anderson recalled a Mrs. Lamont running a Tambouring School in a flat in the old derelict Livingstone mansion to teach girls the craft.

But to turn this small cottage industry into the massive weaving industry it became, huge changes were required, not the least being a massive increase in supplies of raw material. This problem was resolved by replacing flax with plentiful supplies of cotton from America and the West Indies. New technology was also developed to meet the needs of the new industry.

In 1733 John Kay, a Lancashire weaver, invented a way of sending the shuttle automatically to and fro across the loom. This meant that broadcloth could then be woven without an assistant. Then in the 1760s, James Hargreaves, a carpenter and weaver from Blackburn, Lancashire invented a spinning wheel which enabled one person to spin several yarn threads at once by turning a handle. As technology developed more advanced methods were gradually introduced which required water power, and which took the weaving industry into the factories, but that lay in the future.

Given this undreamed of prosperity, and the sense of independence and optimism it engendered, it was only a matter of time before this intelligent class of men addressed the tyrannies that oppressed them, but when the revolt came it was not in the sphere of industry, the explosion erupted in the Kirk.

---

1. *Kilsyth Chronicle* (7th January 1893)
2. Anderson, (Rev.) Robert *A History of Kilsyth and a Memorial of Two Lives*
3. Rennie, (Rev.) Robert *The First Statistical Account of Scotland (Volume IX)*
4. Anderson, (Rev.) Robert ibid.
5. Johnston, Thomas. *Our Scots Noble Families pxxxii* Forward Publishing Co. Ltd. 1909. Republished by Argyll Publishing 1999

CHAPTER 2

ON HALLOWEEN 1517 the German monk Martin Luther had nailed his ninety five Theses to the door of the Castle Church at Wittenberg and ignited the Protestant Revolution which was to change the course of history. Reduced to its essence, the Protestant ethos declared that each person had a direct relationship with God and could interpret the scriptures for themselves without the need of a hierarchical priesthood. The Church should be a priesthood of all believers, as it was described.

Setting aside the theological issues, the political implications, if unintended, were revolutionary. It followed in the minds of many that if in the spiritual sphere each person could strike their own direct relationship with God, with no need of a priesthood or church to mediate, why in the temporal sphere should the people be subject to the 'God given' right of a superior cast of kings and nobleman to rule them at will? This thought and reasoning challenged directly the whole basis of feudal society and spread like wildfire throughout Europe, sparking off the Peasants War in Germany which claimed 100,000 lives; the English Civil War in which 190,000 are estimated to have perished and cost a British king his head. In Scotland it was estimated that 60,000, out of an estimated population of around one million, lost their lives in the various conflicts, not including those who were transported to the plantations in the American colonies.

But when the turmoil died down the ongoing legacy was an endless series of dissensions and secessions from the Church of Scotland. The Rev. Peter Anton was correct on one point; Scots dissent never was against the principles of the Church, but always tended to preserve the old principles of the Church. The frequent schisms had their roots in patronage, in other words – politics. Unlike the English who adopted the Episcopalian model which preserved the power and privileges of the landed aristocracy to appoint clergymen, the Scots adopted Presbyterianism, which did not. The democratic structure of the Kirk was never likely to rest easily with an undemocratic state, and it did not.

This was no abstract matter. The minister who interpreted the Gospels was a massively influential figure, backed by the all-pervasive Church and civil courts. Taken with the practice of that time to interfere and monitor the private lives of everyone in minute detail, so brilliantly satirised by Robert Burns in 'Holy Willie's Prayer', it was regarded as a vital weapon of social control that the minister should be the creature of the landed class, and they fought to retain that power ferociously.

The matter appeared to be finally settled at the union of the Scottish and English parliaments in 1707 when no more interference in the governance of the Church of Scotland was assured. But only four years later, at the behest of the Scottish landlords the Westminster government introduced the Church Patronage (Scotland) Act 1711. Its full title was *an Act to restore the Patrons to their ancient Rights of presenting Ministers to the Churches vacant in that part of Britain called Scotland.*

The Kirk was united in angry opposition which they rightly regarded as a blatant betrayal of a solemn agreement and violation of their faith. The new series of disruptions and secessions which were to follow were not disputes on the issue, but between those who accepted the civil law and those committed to oppose it. It was to continue for over 160 years before the stranglehold of the aristocracy was broken.

Those old Kilsythians being not only devout but knowledgeable of the scriptures and church affairs shared the national anger and resentment at this affront. Yet there is no record of outward opposition when the Rev. John Telfer was presented to the parish in 1753 by King George II. We know little about Mr. Telfer although Anton hints that he was a tough disciplinarian. Farmers were rebuked 'for selling their grass to the Highland drovers at the August tryst on the Sabbath day'. Elders were appointed to go through the town, and challenge and reprove all persons in public houses or wandering idly in the fields. Testimonials were rigorously exacted from all persons taking up residence in the parish. If any employer hired a servant who had not produced a testimonial, and he or she afterwards fell into indigent circumstances, the employer was held liable for his provision. But in truth such authoritarian conduct was not exceptional in that age.

Even under Telfer's sainted predecessor the Rev. James Robe, the records reveal a rigorous diligence in punishing sinners. A woman was brought before the Kirk Session for having on the Lord's Day brought 'a gang of water' from the well; and another person was dealt with for having visited Glasgow on the Sabbath for a secular purpose. It is recorded how a shoemaker was rebuked for having given out from his shop a shoe which he had repaired, and for which he received the price of three half pence, that the owner might be able to attend church.

The most serious punishment was reserved for the big sinners, and there was no bigger sin than fornication. The culprit for three Sabbaths in succession, in token of repentance, had to stand up in his or her seat and before the assembled church, be rebuked and admonished. One Sabbath sufficed if the fault was followed by marriage. (1)

One weaver named Joseph told Robert Anderson years after of his experience. He said:

> 'I couldna staun the public rebuke. If the minister had let me sit
> still in my seat I widna hae minded sae muckle, but whan he
> tell't me tae staun up an the folk turned roon tae glower at me, a
> jist gaed oot at the kirk door, an listed next mornin at the
> Tonteen in Glaska.'

Joseph joined the Scots Greys and nearly lost his life charging Napoleon's Old Guard at Waterloo, before returning to live the rest of his life in Kilsyth.

In earlier times serious sinners faced an even crueler ordeal. The Kilsyth church had its 'cheeks o' branks', a contrivance of iron hoops chained to the church walls which was made to fit the sinner's head, with a spike to enter the mouth and press on the unruly tongue. The sinner had to stand in a 'white sheet' at the church door as the people passed him by, and then sit throughout the service at the 'stool of repentance' placed under the pulpit.

But to return to our narrative, when the crisis came it had little to do with events in Kilsyth but everything to do with the Rev. John Telfer. It arose out of another bitter patronage dispute in another weaving village, Eaglesham six miles south west of Glasgow. In November 1765 the Earl of Eglinton nominated Thomas Clark as the new minister of Eaglesham Parish Church. The parishioners were united in their opposition but the General Assembly ordered the Glasgow Presbytery to carry on with the ordination. In April the following year the Glasgow University Principal along with four ministers and 'a considerable number of gentlemen' accompanied the Rev. Thomas Clark to Eaglesham. (2)

They never reached the church, however. As they approached the village they encountered the wrath of the parishioners:

> 'They were violently attacked by some hundreds of country
> people, men and women, assembled in a tumultuous manner;
> many of the Gentlemen were wounded and bruised with clubs,
> and several of the clergymen beat and insulted, some of the
> chaises cut and broke, and the horses wounded.' (3)

Apparently the party was obliged to retreat in confusion and only outstripped the mob as they ran down towards Clarkston with the good parishioners of Eaglesham 'giving them opprobrious language and pelting them with stones.'

The Presbytery, understandably, were not keen on a speedy return date with the villagers of Eaglesham but the Earl was not going to tolerate any delay. With the despised Patronage Act in his favour, he returned to the General Assembly who ordered the Presbytery to proceed with the ordination; and so on Thursday the 26th June 1766 a Presbytery party returned to Eaglesham, but this time flanked by armed soldiers. The party consisted of the Principal of Glasgow University, one of his professors, one solitary elder and the Rev. John Telfer who had travelled all the way from Kilsyth.

These stirring events were being observed closely in Kilsyth. When challenged by his Kilsyth parishioners Telfer told them to go home and mind their own business. But his parishioners regarded the matter as very much their business. That a minister should be imposed on another weaving community at gunpoint ignited anger, but that their own minister should have volunteered to take part in this obscene ritual was a humiliation too far. The result was 'a numerously signed petition' from the Kilsyth parishioners to the breakaway Relief Presbytery. They claimed the 'people were groaning under oppression,' and asked to be formed into a congregation under that Presbytery's care. The petition was granted and so was set up the first self supporting church in Kilsyth.

As Robert Anderson commented: 'They were a stout-hearted lot. They knew that in cutting themselves off from the State Church they were also cutting themselves off from the State Treasury, but they had counted the cost and were nothing daunted.'

The scale of their ambition was remarkable. They insisted on being described as seceders and not dissenters. This was no minor semantic point. They did not regard themselves as forming a small dissenting sect outwith the main Christian community but were in fact reconstituting the Church of Scotland itself in accordance with its true beliefs and doctrines. This was reflected in the scale of their new church. It was built to accommodate 599 sitters with galleries to be added later, increasing the capacity to 700 sitters. It was in fact similar in its dimensions to the Parish Church then situated at the top of the Howe Road, inside the cemetery. There was, however, one distinctive difference. There was no gallery for the gentry.

But almost as significant as the secession itself was the church they chose as their new spiritual home. The Relief Church which was founded by Thomas Gillespie in 1761, only five years before the Kilsyth secession. This arose out of another patronage dispute when Thomas Gillespie was deposed by the Dunfermline Presbytery for refusing to take part in the settlement of a minister at Inverkeithing. He preached the following day in the churchyard at Carnock, and on following Sundays, first in a neighbouring hollow and then on the public highway, to immense congregations.

When the Relief Presbytery was formed it attracted adherents in many weaving communities, and for good reason. It was much more liberal in outlook than an earlier secession. (4) Though firmly in the Presbyterian tradition, it was less burdened with the stern Calvinistic hell and damnation and other austere mores of the age and influenced by the more relaxed English non-conformists. They even approved of joint services with other denominations. They opened their Communion Tables to all believers, led the way in taking a stand against the evil slave trade, were the first to introduce the hymn book into public worship, a highly contentious issue, and took a lead in sponsoring the foreign missions. (5)

It is easy to understand why such values appealed to weaving communities with their appetite for change and sense of optimism in shaping a new and better future. Indeed, it is estimated that by the 1830s considerably fewer than half of Scottish handloom weavers' families adhered to the established Church. (6)

But there was another more personal reason why the Kilsyth rebels were comfortable with the Relief Church; the Rev. Thomas Gillespie was well known to them. In 1742, some twenty-four years earlier, he was intimately involved in the great Spiritual Revival in Kilsyth which attracted the attention of the nation and beyond. The newly ordained young minister spent a lot of time in Kilsyth helping the parish minister, the Rev. James Robe, and Robe paid full tribute to him. In his book, which was translated into Dutch, Robe wrote that of all his helpers, the Rev. Thomas Gillespie was. . .

> 'most remarkably God's send to me. . . He came to me on the Monday before the Lord's Supper was given in the congregation, and staid ten days. Both of us had much work amongst the distressed as kept us continuously employed from morning to night, and without him, humanely speaking, many of them must have miscarried and continued much longer in their distress.'

It was to be the first of many visits Gillespie was to make to Kilsyth at that time.

There were, and are, two strongly opposed views on the Kilsyth Revival, those who regarded it as a divinely inspired Spiritual Awakening and those who dismiss it as an outburst of mass hysteria. But those who take the negative view have to balance in their judgment that the moderate, progressive and far-sighted Thomas Gillespie did not agree.

Having made their decision, the Kilsyth seceders wasted no time in getting down to business. They sub-feued from an old town feuar a large piece of ground, called in the title deeds 'The Kiln Yard', which was situated at the bottom end of what was to become the Low Craigends. They purchased for a Manse a two-storied house already on the ground, and then began the building of the commodious Meeting House, in which for 125 years God was worshipped until a new church was opened at the Town-foot in January 1893.

The low costs of the time assisted them. They had the whole of their large feu for three shillings and four pence a year. The wages of masons and joiners ran from three to four pence a day. The feu carried with it the right of quarrying freestone in the Garrell Glen, and the farmers did all the carting for nothing.

But they could not have foreseen in their worst nightmares the Baptism of Fire that lay ahead. Tragedy struck early when several masons were working on a roof scaffold which collapsed. One died and two others were described as being 'in a very dangerous case'. (7) It is not difficult to imagine the smug comments of their opponents who had predicted 'that no good would come of it' as they attributed the accident to divine judgment.

But there was no road back for the seceders, not that they were seeking one. They then faced the vital task of appointing a minister for the fledging congregation, and their misfortune continued. Their first appointee lasted only three years. The reason for his resignation is not known but later he became a teacher in Bo'ness, got into trouble through marrying two of his scholars and was banished from Stirlingshire. Their second minister lasted only a year. The reason for his resignation was 'his getting into trouble of a delicate nature which caused him to leave the town'. They fared much better with their third appointment, the Rev. James Dun, a local weaver's son who grew the congregation with sterling service. He served for 12 years until 1792 when he was translated to East Campbell Street Relief Church in Glasgow. He was 'a lad o' pairts', self taught and without wealth or influence he worked his way through college and Divinity Hall, no mean achievement in that age.

But undoubtedly the defining decision of the Relief Church was the inspired appointment in 1793 of a young graduate of Glasgow University who came from the Stirlingshire village of Airth, and who was to serve Kilsyth for 69 years – enter the Rev. John Anderson.

1. Anderson, (Rev.) Robert *A History of Kilsyth and a Memorial of Two Lives*
2. Fraser, (Dr) Brian *A History of the Christian Church in Eaglesham*
3. *Glasgow Journal* (No.1345)
4. Smout, T.C. *A History of the Scottish People 1560-1830* p.217
5. Struthers, (Rev) Gavin *A History of the Relief Church*
6. Murray, Norman *The Scottish Handloom Weavers 1790-1850*
7. *Evening Courant* (22nd October 1768)

CHAPTER 3

HAVING GOT THEIR LINKS with heaven secure, the remainder of the 1790s saw the weavers grow in numbers, prosperity, confidence and ambition. By 1796, out of a total Kilsyth workforce of nearly one thousand, almost 700 were employed in the textile industry. But though its impact was not immediate it is important to our narrative to recognise another phenomenon which had taken place in the second half of the century – the Scottish Enlightenment – arguably the greatest flowering of intellectual talent in one unlikely and concentrated area the world has known.

Centred in Edinburgh and Glasgow, Scottish thinkers, scientists and artists such as Adam Smith, David Hume, Francis Hutcheson, Robert Burns, James Hutton and many others were doing nothing less than defining the modern world in subjects ranging over philosophy, economics, architecture, medicine, law, chemistry, social science and many others. Sharing the commitment of the European Enlightenment to rational humanism, the Scots movement had its special flavour in its empiricism and practicality with the chief virtues held to be improvement, virtue and practical benefit for both the individual and society.

For good reason these Scottish thinkers were called the 'moral sense' philosophers. They believed human beings are both moral and sociable creatures, and that society is not ultimately based on rational self-interest, but rather in our innate feelings of human sympathy. (1.) Most of these remarkable trailblazers knew each other well and drank, debated and socialised together as well as helping each other in their pioneering work. Once when the king's chemist was in town he said: 'Here I stand at what is called the Cross of Edinburgh, and can in a few minutes shake fifty men of genius by the hand.'

It was not such a big exaggeration. It was all the more remarkable that this epoch-changing event should be taking place in what was regarded as a small, poor, backward country on the northern fringe of Europe which was only recently ravaged by the Jacobite wars. Even Voltaire was moved to remark, 'We now look to Scotland for all our ideas of civilisation.'

It can take some time for ideas conceived in seats of learning to percolate down to life in the streets, but in Scotland the process took place more quickly due to the strong support of the Church for universal education, and the consequent democratic basis of education which allowed clever students of modest means, such as the Rev. John Anderson, into the universities.

But access to knowledge was not made easy. We know that those Kilsyth weavers absorbed and debated endlessly all books they could get their hands on, but were legislated out of access to information on what was going on in the world around them. The instrument was the notorious Newspaper Tax, which the radicals accurately named a 'tax on knowledge', which ensured that only the rich could benefit from this emerging medium of communication. The tax was introduced in 1712 and lasted around a century and a half. There was no disagreement on its purpose. The Government stated that the stamp duty was designed to stop the publication of newspapers and pamphlets that tended to 'excite hatred and contempt for the government and holy religion.'

The radical, Richard Carlile did not dispute the lines of battle. He wrote in his publication *The Republican:*

'Let us then continue to progress in knowledge, since knowledge is demonstrably proved to be power. It is the power of knowledge that checks the crimes of cabinets and courts; it is the power of knowledge that must put a stop to bloody wars.' (2)

For refusing to pay the stamp duty Carlile was found guilty of blasphemy and seditious libel and sentenced to three years in Dorchester Gaol. Undeterred he continued to direct his newspaper from behind prison walls through his wife, Jane, and sister, Mary, but within a year they joined him in prison on two year sentences. Carlile then appealed for volunteers to sell *The Republican*. The establishment *Morning Chronicle* pointed out that Carlile was bound to fail as 'we can hardly conceive that mere attachment to any set of principles without any hope of gain or advantage will induce men to expose themselves to imprisonment for three years'.

They were wrong. Over the next few years over 150 men and women were sent to prison for selling *The Republican*. They served a total of over 200 years. Many others were to follow. It is often forgotten that newspaper freedom was a vital plank in the campaign for democracy, and, as so often, it was waged by ordinary men and women who were called on to pay a heavy price.

The measures to choke off the information, the oxygen of democracy, was felt deeply in Kilsyth as elsewhere. Around a century later Robert Anderson wrote:

'. . . it is difficult to conceive of a community without any
newspapers at all. This, however, was virtually the condition of
Kilsyth at the beginning of the century. The 'weeklies' and there
were no other kind, hardly had a circulation where they were
published, and they were expensive. No wonder. They had a
heavy Government tax to pay, which was not repealed till 1885,
and there was the paper duty besides, which was not taken off
till 1861. There was not a paper to be got under four and a half
pence. To get one even at that was no small difficulty in country
towns like Kilsyth. Richer folks might manage it, but the people
generally were without newspapers. Though not extra rich my
father had one. It was a belated sheet. At the end of this century
we could read about what happened, say at Modder River, in
South Africa, more than 6,000 miles away, and know all about
the battle before the mortally wounded were all dead. At the end
of last century when the Continental War was going on, it took
weeks to get tidings about anything from abroad. There was the
long sea voyage of the sailing ship, bringing dispatches from
Alexandria, telling what Nelson was doing at the Nile, or from
Lisbon or Madrid, telling what Wellington was doing on the

Duro. There was the deliberation of the Cabinet about publishing the dispatches in the 'Times'. Then London knew but not the nation. The trotting coaches then set out for the English towns, and they knew. In due time they got across the borders into Scotland, and Edinburgh and Glasgow knew. A sail boat across the Irish Channel for Dublin, and it knew. It was comparatively the Dark Ages. When my father did, at last, get the news, rumours ran through the town, and there was a big audience on the Sabbath. It was from the pulpit the eager crowd heard about Camperdown, Cape St. Vincent, the Nile and Trafalgar, together with all the Peninsular victories, till Napoleon, after Waterloo, was shut up in St. Helena.

About 1820 newspaper clubs began, each member reading in the order agreed on, and getting an hour to do it. These were second-hand readers at a cheap rate, and it was a poor rag of a newspaper before all was done.'

If access to current news was difficult, the issue of general education was another matter. The Scottish handloom weavers in the late 1700s were regarded as the best educated working class group in the whole of Europe, and the Kilsyth weavers were arguably ahead of most Scottish communities. The passion for education had its roots in the Reformation, and particularly in the doctrine of the 'priesthood of all the faithful'. It followed that if each individual had to strike his own direct relationship with God, it was necessary to inform his conscience and judgment, and that meant having the ability to read in order to absorb and interpret the Bible.

The Scottish parliament had passed several Acts to provide a national education system, including the 1696 Act which required the heritors, local landowners, to provide at least one school in each parish along with the meagre salary for a teacher and a house. But as one historian pointed out, 'never was there a wiser law, and never was a law more studiously disregarded.' (3) The landowners, true to character, found ways of evading their responsibility, and the provision of education was frequently left to unfunded local ministers and other enthusiasts. Gaps in provision were often filled by 'adventure schools' which were poorly equipped and staffed private schools which charged a fee.

Although the principle of education for all was frequently dishonoured and was often observed more in the breach than the observance, nevertheless Scottish education was unique in that all the way back to the Education Act of 1496 this was the only country since Sparta in ancient Greece to be committed in principle to a system of general public education.

Several factors combined to put Kilsyth ahead in education provision, not least the white knight who came to the aid of the parish. He was not a local landowner but a local boy made good. John Patrick who had risen to become a successful London merchant left the Kirk Session a bequest of £60, the interest to go towards the fees of any poor children connected with the district. To the credit of the Kirk Session, the trustees of the fund, they invested wisely increasing the fund to £500. The school at Chapel Green built in 1723 meant that throughout the Golden Age of the weavers they had a well equipped school with highly qualified teachers.

Another boost to local education came through the efforts of the Rev. John Anderson. It was noted earlier how he lent out his own books to parishioners. This was to lead to the setting up of a church library which accumulated a remarkable stock of 800 books, and eventually the service was opened to all citizens of the town for a small fee.

It is little wonder that William Anderson's biographer should state that the handloom weavers of Kilsyth, where William was raised, were 'a very intelligent and a very Radical Class'. (4) William, Robert's older brother, was to become the most famous of all the Andersons. He was very much a product of his family and community, and his reputation as a preacher and political campaigner was to extend far beyond the borders of Scotland. He was a pupil at Chapel Green in the early years of the 1800s.

The story is told of how when he went to Chapel Green he found he was the only boy who wore shoes and stockings. When he left the manse in the morning he took off his shoes and stockings and hid them in a hedge as he did not want to be the only 'booted' boy in the class. William had, of course, the advantage of being taught at home by his father, but it is interesting to note that when he went to Chapel Green along with a dozen other local scholars they had all been taught at home in the basics of English reading, writing and arithmetic and were now ready to study Latin, Greek and other advanced subjects.

William Anderson went on to Glasgow University where he was a distinguished scholar. In 1822 he was ordained as the minister of the Relief John Street Church in Glasgow which was in a reduced state with a dwindling congregation. He not only filled the church but had it demolished and rebuilt. It was there he built his reputation and remained until his retirement. His preaching which electrified his congregation was said to have been delivered in a pronounced Kilsyth accent, which would have been more distinctive at that time. He had inherited his grandfather's resolute boldness and no subject was out of bounds or any controversy within his Church or society in general avoided as he imposed in plain candid language a Christian perspective on the issue of the day. When he was not expounding from his pulpit he was addressing packed audiences in the City Hall on political issues such as anti-slavery, political reform, the iniquitous Corn Laws and issues of human liberty at home and abroad. He had, of course, many critics who objected to his frank political discourses. They did not deter him for a moment. In one sermon he roundly denounced passive obedience and non-resistance. He said:

> 'There are some preachers who presume to inculcate that it is unbecoming of Christians to take part in political disputes, and they will prostitute the Scriptures in their advocacy in their perpetuation of abuses calling upon us to meddle not with them that are given to change, as if all desire of change implied a discontentedness of disposition which nothing will satisfy. Those declaimers against politics will usually be found to be themselves the most violent political partisans in the defence of corruption, that it be allowed to fester undisturbed. It is impracticable to dissociate the history of patriotism in this country from the history of a Reformed Church.'

But the topic of education provides a stark reminder that the pursuit of democracy was not a theoretical exercise divorced from consequences in the real world, and that government unaccountable to the people it governs is almost by definition corrupt.

Let us fast forward from the end of the 1700s, to 1872 when the government took control of education to attempt equity of provision throughout the country. A board of Government placemen was set up to implement the Education Act in Scotland, with responsibility then passing to the Education Department in London. In a piece of shameless gerrymandering they split the Kilsyth parish into two School Boards, one covering the landward area where the landlords and their friends lived, and the other for the burgh. They even altered the burgh boundaries to ensure their friends were included in the landward area. They then allocated all the school properties and all the funding to the landward board, even the existing Burngreen School which was in the burgh. Even when the public purse was financing services, the landlords were still in power, and continued shamelessly to abuse their powers in their own interests.

Robert Anderson was elected chairman of the Burgh Board and they made a plea to the Scotch Education Department urging that in terms of commonsense and fair play one school board should provide for all children in the parish as the vast majority of the children were within the burgh, with a negligible number in the landward area. They also protested at the unfairness of giving the Landward Board, which had little to do, 'all the money and property, and nothing at all to the Burgh Board, on which rested the burden of education outlay and work'.

After a long delay the Department replied, rejecting all their requests. The Burgh Board then asked that at least they be given the Burngreen School and schoolhouse which was 'useless to the Landward Board'. They were then summoned to Edinburgh and told there would be no change, and were more or less given a dressing down for their impertinence. Deprived of resources they then set out to provide education for 600 children. They managed to rent a disused factory in the Beggar's Close which they cleaned and fitted out as best they could. They then attempted to find a site for a new school. They tried for a field below Dovecotwood with entry from the Quarry Road; they then tried for a site at Inns Park and after that they sought a site in a rising field to the south of what was to become the Burns Church with entry from Howe Road. All applications were turned down. They eventually were offered by the Edmonstones the most unattractive site in the town, a field in the Craigends which was useless for any other purpose. Not only was it too small but was covered by jutting rocks that would have to be removed before building could commence. Fortunately, local men who worked in the quarries were able to dynamite the rock and prepare the site, and so the Kilsyth Academy was built.

But the Edmonstones were not finished. Adding insult to injury they insisted that for legal reasons they would have to pay for the ground. The heritors not only frustrated the educational purpose of the Act, they managed also to achieve a profit. Robert Anderson concluded that 'comment was tempting but what's the use?' The coolness of the Edmonstones towards universal education, however, may have had a more profound cause. Sir Archibald Edmonstone had opposed educating the poor people of Ireland and India on the grounds that 'neither people were likely to benefit from it, and widespread literacy would lead to a contagion of dangerous ideas among the lower classes.' (5)

1. Sacks, Jonathon *Politics of Hope* (Foreword by Gordon Brown)
2. *Republican* (4th October 1820)
3. Doyle, Margaret B.S. *The Provision of education in Kilsyth'1760-1915* Jordanhill College of Education, 1973
4. Gilfillan, George *Life of the Rev. William Anderson* London Hodder and Stoughton
5. McVey, David *Scottish Local History* Issue 81 p38

CHAPTER 4

BY NECESSITY, the thoughts, actions and aspiration of those Kilsyth weavers were shrouded in secrecy. The best insight is gained by considering the people they read and supported, and two figures loomed large in the their thoughts; one player on the international stage, Thomas Paine, and the other of national, and even local renown, Thomas Muir of Huntershill.

By any standard the rise and fame of Thomas Paine was extraordinary. A poor corset maker from Thetford in England who emigrated to America, and after almost stumbling into journalism was to shake the world to its foundations. His pamphlet *Common Sense*, which was published by Robert Bell, an emigrant Scotsman, almost on its own galvanised Americans into fighting and winning their independence and then going on to establish a democratic republic. The doubts and timidity of those American settlers were swept away by the force and clarity of Paine's denunciation of corrupt royal and aristocratic government. He urged his new fellow countrymen to shape the future with a new democratic republic.

'We have within our power to begin the world over again. . . the building of a new world is at hand,' he wrote.

Within three months 130,000 copies were sold and discussed wherever Americans met. Editions were published in many countries abroad, including one in Edinburgh. In all, 500,000 copies were sold, the largest sale in those days of any publication after the Bible. In the view of one American historian, it was 'the most brilliant pamphlet written during the American Revolution, and one of the most brilliant pamphlets ever written in the English language.' (1)

It was the genius of Thomas Paine to recognise the links between convulsions going on in three countries – The American War of Independence, the French Revolution, and the campaign for reform in Britain which was to lead to the great 1832 Reform Act. He recognised and explained they were three parts of the same whole. Each reacted on the other and each is incomprehensible without the other.

Having played a major and noble role in winning America's freedom and forming its democratic constitution, Paine returned to Britain. He took a room in the Angel Inn in Islington and settled down to write *The Rights of Man*, which was to strike the weavers in Kilsyth and elsewhere like a thunderbolt. All those inchoate ideas, grievances and aspirations were brought together in a lucid plan to create a new social order. Published in two parts, the first was essentially a stinging rebuke of Edmond Burke's attack on the French Revolution and his defence of the divine right of Royal government. Paine scathingly dismissed hereditary power as being as absurd as a hereditary mathematician or a hereditary poet laureate. He held that the dead could not hold dominion over the living and argued that only a democratic republic could be trusted to defend the freedom and rights of all the people.

That long and detailed debate can still be read today with interest, and though Thomas Paine was driven into exile for his contribution it was a debate he won. Progressive countries all over the world have moved in the direction set out by Thomas Paine, not Edmond Burke, and even modern-day tyrants and dictators are obliged to pay at least lip service to the democratic norms and principles declared by Paine.

Having demonstrated that the economic and social order the weavers craved and needed was achievable he went on in Part Two of *The Rights of Man* to map out a concept they must have found electrifying; it was nothing less than the welfare state.

Since that period in our nation's history was recently disinterred and came under public gaze, historians have split fiercely, as historians do, on the question of were those weavers revolutionary or too subservient? Reading what the weavers were saying, at least at the time we are considering, they were merely seeking reasonable reform. They were proud of their new status and potential, and had no wish to return to a life of rural subservience. That probably explains why Luddite activities such as the wrecking of machinery never took hold in Scotland. They merely sought an economic and social order consistent with family and community life where they could develop their skills and ply their trade with some protection from the arbitrary ravages of free-market forces which visited on them such misery.

Paine's proposals provided the answer. His plan included old age pensions, progressive taxation geared to income, family allowances, maternity benefits, a system of free education, prison reform. This was not just a wish list. He produced a blueprint detailing how it could be organised and costed. It was to be over two hundred years and into the twentieth century before we began to catch up with Paine's vision. As Labour Party leader, Michael Foot put it, 'Much of the future the Labour Party has offered was previously on offer, in even better English, from Thomas Paine.' (2)

The British establishment were apoplectic, but Paine's fearless belief in freedom of thought and expression, for himself and everyone, blinded him from the growing danger. On 13th September 1792 he was about to leave a friend's house when none other than the poet William Blake told him, 'You must not go home or you are a dead man.' Convinced, Paine set out immediately for Dover. The order to arrest him on a charge of seditious libel, which carried the death penalty, reached Dover just twenty minutes after he boarded the ship that was to take him to France. He was tried in his absence and outlawed, and was never again to set foot on British soil.

The genie, however, was out of the bottle. *The Rights of Man* sold a staggering 200,000 copies in England, Wales and Scotland and 100,000 copies in America. It was translated into Gaelic. Robert Burns, a keen observer and supporter of the American Revolution, added his own genius to many of the novel and radical themes of Paine. Like many other poets of the age, his most famous political songs could not be published under his name. *A Man's a Man for a' That* and *Scots Wha Hae* were seditious, even traitorous. To hold democratic views was to be a traitor. In *The Rights of Woman* Burns diced with danger. He wrote:

> While Europe's eye is fix'd on mighty things,
> The fate of empires and the fall of kings;
> While quacks of State must each produce his plan,

And even children lisp the Rights of Man;
Amid this mighty fuss just let me mention,
The Rights of Woman merit some attention.

The great odyssey of Thomas Paine continued in France where he was celebrated as a hero of liberty. He had French citizenship conferred on him by the French Assembly of which he was to become a distinguished member. Yet, within a year as the Revolution descended into the Reign of Terror he was to find himself in prison facing execution. His crime was to plead for the life of King Louis XVI. How ironical, yet typical, that the greatest scourge of monarchy should plead for the life of a king, though he knew that in voting for the King's life he was voting for his own death.

Yet, in the shadow of the guillotine, with death seeming imminent, he sat down to write another explosive tract. *The Age of Reason* was an unrelenting attack on all revealed religion, particularly state-sponsored religion, which he regarded as an instrument of oppression and tyranny and an affront to reason.

Weak and ill, he was eventually released from prison but it was not until 1802 that he returned to America after a fifteen years absence. Nothing could have prepared him for the reception he received from the citizens of the Republic which he had done so much to create. If Thomas Muir and the Scottish weavers were finessed out of the history books, Tom Paine was driven out in a venomous campaign of hatred, bigotry and ignorance. *The Age of Reason* was the cause. Those who were unwilling or unable to engage with his arguments found any other means, true or false, to castigate the 'infidel'. From every pulpit and platform he was denounced. The fury of the religious was a useful shield for his many other enemies, the slave owners, the ex-royalists and those who for their own gain had attempted to compromise the Revolution.

No slander or insult was too vile to be heaped on his head. He was stopped from riding on a coach. As H.N. Brailsford put it, 'the grandsons of the Puritan Colonists who had flogged Quaker women as witches denied him a place on the stagecoach lest an offended God should strike it with lightening.' Three years before his death in June

1809 he suffered the indignity of being stopped at the polling booth when he went to cast his vote. He, who was the first to utter the words the 'United States of America' was denied the vote on the false grounds that he was not an American citizen.

His funeral was attended only by a Quaker watchmaker, a French woman friend with her two young sons, and walking behind were two black men who had walked twenty-two miles to honour the man who had raised the standard against slavery and refused to allow it to be lowered.

But even a century later Theodore Roosevelt would dismiss him as 'a dirty little atheist'. He was wrong on all three accounts, significantly the latter; Paine was not an Atheist, he was a Deist. However, Michael Foot was probably correct in saying that Paine would have agreed with Cato's comment that he would prefer people should ask why he had not a monument erected to him than why he had. One great American, Thomas Jefferson, always recognised Paine's contribution to American democracy despite the torrent of abuse.

It has taken two centuries to wipe away the mud. As the enormity of Paine's contribution to America and humanity re-emerges, more Americans have come to the view of another President, John Adams, that 'the United Stated of America was born as much from the pen of Thomas Paine as it was from the sword of George Washington.' As late as 1898 America's greatest ever defence lawyer, Clarence Darrow, was defending trade union officials charged with criminal conspiracy for organising a woodworkers strike. The prosecution cited in its cause an old case where a man was convicted and imprisoned for writing favourably about Thomas Paine. Darrow, who was always more interested in justice than law, turned the reference into a withering attack on the convicting jury and the State. He told the jury. 'Why, if the names of that jury were blazoned upon the wall of this court of justice today even the prosecutor would turn and view them with contempt. . . this prosecutor would have you go back to those trials of 100 years ago when they convicted a man for writing poetry dedicated to liberty and common sense. They convicted him, gentlemen, because he wrote a poem lauding Thomas Paine and his *Rights of Man*. They convicted him because he said a word in favour of a man who perhaps did as much for American liberty and universal liberty than any man who ever lived.' (3)

It was not an accident that in the recent inauguration speech of the first African American president he should quote the words of Thomas Paine. As his speech moved towards its climax Barrack Obama said:

> 'So let as mark this day with remembrance of who we are and how far we have travelled. In the year of America's birth, in the coldest of months, a small band of patriots huddled by dying campfires on the shores of an icy river. The capital was abandoned. The enemy was advancing. The snow was stained with blood. At a moment when the outcome of our revolution was most in doubt, the father of our nation ordered these words to be read to the people. 'Let it be told to the future world that in the depth of winter, when nothing but hope and virtue could survive, that the city and the country, alarmed at one common danger, came forth to meet it.' '

These stirring words were written by Thomas Paine in the pamphlet *American Crisis* and ordered by George Washington to be read to his troops before they crossed the Delaware River at Christmas in 1776 to do battle with King George's Hessian mercenaries encamped at Trenton. The disheartened soldiers, ragged, barefoot, half frozen and half starved took up their muskets again and the battle of Trenton was won. Not surprisingly the *American Crisis* was ordered to be burned by the public hangman in England.

Let us leave Thomas Paine with the judgment of H.R. Brailsford:

> 'The neglected pioneer of one revolution, the honoured victim of another, brave to the point of folly, and as humane as he was brave, no man in his generation preached republican virtue in better English, nor lived with finer disregard of self.'

---

1. *The Freeman* (January 1996)
2. Foot, Michael *Debts of Honour*
3. Weinberg, Arthur (editor) *Attorney for the Damned* (University of Chicago Press)

CHAPTER 5

AT THE TIME of Thomas Paine's flight to France, the cause of democratic reform inflamed the country. What was required was political leadership. It may seem strange that it should be Thomas Muir, a talented and idealistic young advocate who should step up to the plate to fulfil that role. It is important to recognise the differences as well as the similarities between Muir and Paine. Muir was not converted to democratic reform by Paine but at Glasgow University where the ideas of the Scottish Enlightenment were challenging the old order. Neither was Muir a revolutionary. Though he was in sympathy with the American and French Revolutions he firmly believed that Britain could and would be reformed by constitutional means, namely public campaigns and pressure, and not by importing revolutionary ideas and assistance from abroad. It is also worthy of note that Muir, unlike Paine, was a committed Christian and Presbyterian and remained so all his life.

In fact there had been pressure for reform, both Burgh and Parliamentary, from many sections of society for some years. As feudalism gave way to the new industrial age the middle class leaders of the new order also growingly resented the monopoly hold on power of the aristocratic landowners who continued to rule in their own interests.

Thomas Muir's father, James, was the younger son of a 'bonnet' laird, roughly the equivalent of a better off tenant farmer, based at Birdston, just around three miles from Kilsyth. James entered the hop trade with the help of English relatives and set up a successful shop in Glasgow's High Street. Thomas was born above the shop in 1765, literally on the doorstep of Glasgow University, which was then situated on the east side of the High Street. When fourteen years old he enrolled at the junior section of the university.

Scottish education was then remarkably egalitarian with the sons of aristocrats being taught alongside the middle class and a number of poor children. To save money, many would walk long distances to the city bringing a bag of oatmeal to sustain them during the term. Just as the industrial revolution was bringing rapid change and expansion to Glasgow, the Scottish Enlightenment was generating conflicts within the university as the new breed of brilliant intellectuals clashed with the old fashioned professors appointed by Tory patronage, and who were resistant to change of any kind.

Thomas Muir was not alone in falling under the influence of one of the most brilliant teachers of the new breed, Prof. John Millar, who made Glasgow Law School internationally famous and is regarded as one of the world's first sociologists. Millar had been a student of Adam Smith and David Hume, and his radical convictions were to shape the values and careers of many of his students, including Thomas Muir. Millar believed that power and law were usually manipulated in the interest of minorities, not for the welfare of all. He supported the American War of Independence and the anti-slavery campaign. He was a firm advocate of both burgh and parliamentary reform and an opponent of church patronage. Even after being appointed as a professor he appeared free of charge as counsel for poor people, as Thomas Muir was also to do later. It was Prof. Millar who persuaded Muir to switch from studying divinity to law, but it was another rebellious giant, Prof. John Anderson, who was to bring about Muir's expulsion from Glasgow University.

Prof. Anderson was a thorn in the flesh of the old order, critical of their incompetence and neglect of students' educational interests. He wanted to break down barriers to knowledge and attempted to interest artisans in science, making his lectures open to everyone. When the faculty eventually suspended him from all exercise of academic discipline the students rebelled and appealed to the university's Lord Rector, who was none other than Edmund Burke. When Burke refused to support them, the students took their revenge by not re-electing him. This infuriated the establishment who prevented Burke's rejection by threats and intimidation. They ordered that the ringleaders, of whom Muir was one of the most prominent, were not to be admitted to classes until they apologised and there was an official inquiry. Muir refused to apologise and was expelled.

However, his career was saved when through the intervention of Prof. Millar he was offered a place at Edinburgh University, where after two years further study he qualified as an advocate, being called to the bar in 1787, aged twenty-two. As for Prof. Anderson, he got his revenge over the old order. In his will he left all his property and apparatus to set up a new educational establishment to be run on lines he outlined. This was the Anderson College which was to become Strathclyde University.

Meanwhile, Muir was not long in building up a good reputation and healthy legal practice, at the same time as he stepped up his campaign for political reform. He made important connections through his legal friends with Whig reformers in Edinburgh and then in London. On a visit to London he was warmly welcomed by the Society of the Friends of the People, a reform society set up by young well-to-do Whigs. Muir was convinced that a new reform movement was needed in Scotland, and he became the inspiration and driving force behind the Scottish Society of the Friends of the People. The first branch was established in Edinburgh and soon branches mushroomed in cities, towns and villages throughout Scotland.

There was one vital difference between the London Society and its sister movement in Scotland; the Scottish Society embraced people of all backgrounds and occupations. Muir frequently made the fifteen hour coach journey from Edinburgh to Glasgow to represent clients and recruit reformers. He held clandestine meetings with groups of weavers and bleach-field workers in Campsie, Kirkintilloch, Lennox-town and Paisley. There is no record of him speaking in Kilsyth, but given his close associations with the town and the fact that Kilsyth had a 'very active branch of the Friends of the People' it is most likely that he did.

The question is why was Thomas Muir singled out by the Government for oppression? The answer lies partly in Muir's strategy and partly by the unfortunate turn of events in France which left the reformers somewhat isolated. He believed the campaign for democracy should include men of all classes and become an all-British movement.

That is why he befriended the United Irishmen, a reform society formed largely of professional men in Dublin and Belfast, called United because Protestants and Catholics combined to demand a more representative Irish Parliament. One of their members, James Hope, expressed their aim and objects in song.

> Och, Paddies, me hearties, have done wid your Parties
> Let min of all creeds and professions agree,
> If Orange and Green, min, no longer were seen, min,
> Ahh, nacboclis, how aisy ould Ireland we'd free

The Government were concerned when the first Convention of the Delegates of the Scottish Friends of the People was held over two days in Edinburgh in December 1792, with 160 delegates representing 80 societies from 35 towns and villages. They were even more concerned when Muir presented an address of support from the United Irishmen. But the overarching crime in their eyes was that Muir was for the first time bringing into political action ordinary working men.

If there was any doubt, the infamous Lord Braxfield clearly spelt it out later at Muir's trial. He lambasted Muir for going about. . .

> 'among ignorant country people and among the lower classes,
> making them leave their work, and inducing them to believe
> that reform was absolutely necessary for preserving their
> liberty, which, had it not been for him, they never would have
> suspected was in danger.'

Then turning on Muir's witnesses, mostly weavers and ordinary working people from this area, he said,

> 'What right had they to representation? Parliament would
> never listen to their petition. Government, in this country is
> made up of the landed interest, which alone has a right to be
> represented; as for the rabble, who have nothing but personal
> property, what hold has the nation of them. . .'

This was the typical gratuitous abuse that those intelligent patriotic weavers had to bear in those pre-democratic times. They had to listen to themselves described by Edmund Burke as 'the swinish herd'. One of the few occasions during his trial when Muir displayed anger was when the Lord Advocate sneered at Muir, 'a gentleman, a member of the Bar', for associating with one of his witnesses, Barclay, 'an ignorant old countryman,' who was an Elder of the Kirk at Cadder. Muir rose to his feet. He said,

> 'I tell the Lord Advocate, the aristocracy of Scotland, I glory more in the friendship of such an old, poor and virtuous man, than in the friendship of the highest titled peer, who derives the source of his guilty grandeur from the calamities of the people, who wrings out a splendid but miserable revenue from their sorrow and distress which he squanders in dissipation.'

It could be said that if Keir Hardie was the founder of the Labour Party, Thomas Muir was the founder of the Labour Movement in Scotland. His biographer, and distant relative, Christina Bewley, put it more modestly: 'Muir was helping to lay the basis of the first working men's clubs, to create the foundation of a labour movement in Scotland.' (1)

Even before the Edinburgh Convention in 1792 dark menacing clouds were blowing over from France. Their royal family were imprisoned and in September a republic was proclaimed. Under the Jacobins the massacres of prisoners which followed deeply shocked the British people, and signs of French imperial expansion changed the public mood.

It was all too easy for the British Government to equate the reformers with the French revolutionaries though there was not the slightest evidence for doing so. It is impossible to find a speech or document by Muir or the other reform leaders in which they did not warn against any unruly or unconstitutional conduct; they even offered to assist the authorities in quelling any disorder. The reformers pledged their loyalty to Britain and sought unity through moderate reform, but their voice was drowned out in the anti-French hysteria.

Illustrious Martyr in the glorious cause
Of truth, of freedom, and of equal laws.

Thomas Muir of Huntershill, the father of Scottish democracy who had strong connections with Kilsyth

Robert Anderson described the feeling among the weavers in Kilsyth at the time. 'All minor causes of social discord, all political unrest ceased in the presence of this danger. The radicals were all patriots, and this was not the time to discuss their rights and wrongs, not till the French business was seen to and settled.'

He tells how men in numbers forsook their looms, bade farewell to the banks and braes of the Garrel, enlisted in the barrack yards of Glasgow and Stirling; and in the ranks of the Forty-Second, and astride the horses of the Scots Greys, the first troop which was said to be mustered in the Burngreen, they, under Sir John Moore and Wellington, fought the French on many a battlefield. Some of them never came back.

It was in this context and against this background that Burns wrote these much misunderstood lines.

Be Britain still to Britain true,
Amang oursels united!
For never but by British hands
Must British wrangs be righted!

> ... Who will not sing God save the King
> Shall hang as high as the steeple;
> But while we sing God save the King
> We will never forget the People!

It was a forlorn attempt by Burns to make the reasonable case that there was no conflict between reform and patriotism.

In this changing public mood many of the leading Whigs and influential middle class reformers quietly withdrew from the scene. The time was right for the government to strike. On 2nd January 1793, less than a month after the Edinburgh Convention, Thomas Muir was travelling to Edinburgh to represent a client. When his coach stopped at the Holytown stage post he was arrested by a king's messenger and taken before a sheriff in Edinburgh. Muir was asked if he had ever given anyone copies of Paine's works, or of the *Patriot*, a radical magazine which the Government alleged Muir had circulated mainly around Kirkintilloch. He exercised his legal right by refusing to answer any questions, and in turn sought the identity of his informers as he had been 'credibly assured' that certain people had been promised places and emoluments if they gave evidence against him.

A few days after being released on bail Muir travelled to London to meet leading reformers and address 'Friends of the Liberty of the Press.' He told them: 'Liberty of the press and free speech in Scotland were almost at an end. Spies intruded into all company, sentinels of the Treasury were stationed in every tavern, rewards offered to informers.'

He then made the fateful decision to cross to France for a short visit, planning to return to Edinburgh for his trial when a date was fixed. But on February 1st France declared war on Britain and due to a ship embargo it was not possible for him to return to Scotland. His trial fixed for 11th February was adjourned to the 25th, but when he was still unable to return he was outlawed.

His father urged him in a letter not to return but to go to America until things cooled down, but Muir was not fully aware how the situation had deteriorated. Three printers who had drunk a toast of 'damnation to all crowned heads' were sentenced to nine months imprisonment. Publishers of reform literature were arrested and others took flight to America. Muir, however, felt it a matter of honour that he should return to Scotland and defend himself and his cause. Eventually he boarded the American ship *The Hope* which was sailing for Baltimore via Belfast. On embarking at Belfast he travelled to Dublin and spent a week being entertained by his friends, the United Irishmen. On 30th July *The Hope* crossed the North Channel and Muir transferred to a small boat which carried him to Port Patrick. He was quickly recognised, arrested and imprisoned at Stranraer. On Sunday August 4th he was clapped in handcuffs and leg-irons and taken to Edinburgh. (2)

Amongst the crowds lining the pavements as Muir passed through the village of Gatehouse in chains was Robert Burns. He returned to his lodgings and completed *Scots Wha Hae* which was to become Scotland's unofficial national anthem

> By Oppression's woes and pains!
> By your Son's in servile chains!
> We will drain our dearest veins,
> But they shall be free!
> Lay the proud Usurpers low
> Tyrants fall in every foe!
> LIBERTY'S in every blow!
> Let us Do – or Die!!!

As Burns wrote to a friend, 'the anthem was inspired by the glowing ideas of some other struggles, not quite so ancient.' The poem was published anonymously to coincide with Muir's trial. The poet was taking a frightful risk. He had already been investigated for sedition, and if he were to be fired from his job with the Customs and Excise his family would be driven into destitution. He was also well aware that in the vindictive climate of the time an even more horrific fate could befall him. That is why in his anxiety he hid his political books, which included the works of Paine, in the house of George Haugh, a Dumfries tinsmith.

The trial of Thomas Muir began in Edinburgh on a stormy, miserable day on 30th August 1793. It lasted sixteen hours and left an indelible blot on Scottish legal history. The indictment charged him with exciting disaffection by seditious speeches, advising and exhorting persons to purchase and persue seditious and wicked publications and circulating various seditious papers, particularly *The Rights of Man*. The jury was rigged, consisting of Government employees and members of the Goldsmiths Hall Association, an anti-reform organisation which had offered rewards for evidence of anyone circulating Paine's work. Even reading the sanitised transcript of the trial today it is obvious the whole process was a gross perversion of justice. To one juryman, Horner, as he passed behind the bench, Lord Braxfield whispered, 'Come awa' Maister Horner, and help us to hang ane a' thae damned scoundrels.' Throughout the trial he treated Muir with brutality and arrogance and bullied his witnesses, many who were poor people from the Kilsyth district.

In his address to the jury Muir said,

> 'Gentleman of the jury, this is perhaps the last time that I shall address my country. . . from my infancy to this moment, I have devoted myself to the cause of the people. It is a good cause – it shall ultimately prevail – it shall finally triumph. Say then, openly, in your verdict, if you do condemn me, which I presume you will not, that it is for my attachment to this cause alone, and not for those vain and wretched pretexts, stated in the indictment, intended only to colour and disguise the real motives of my accusation.'

The following day the sentence of fourteen years' transportation to Botany Bay was handed down. Even the rigged jury was appalled and agreed the sentence was too severe.

Transportation at that time was as close to a death sentence as you could get. Many ships sank on the voyage, and many convicts died of dysentery or typhoid on the journey or from the harsh conditions they faced in Australia. On the voyage to Botany Bay as many as a quarter could die before even reaching there, and half as many again after landing. (3) When sentence was passed Muir said, 'I shall not animadvert on the severity or leniency of my sentence. . . my mind tells me that I have engaged in a good, a just, and a glorious cause, a cause which sooner or later must and will prevail; and by a timely reform, save this country from destruction.'

The savagery of the sentence sent shock waves throughout Europe. A German journalist wrote that the trial 'must excite in the breast of every German an esteem for his native land. We here see a man sent to Botany Bay on account of an accusation to which a German court of justice would have been ashamed to listen.'

But the Government was not finished. Four other leading reformers were tried in Scotland and transported. The Rev. Thomas Fyshe Palmer, a Cambridge-educated Unitarian minister from Dundee; Maurice Margarot, a wine merchant, and the only one to return to his native shores; Joseph Gerrald, a barrister, and William Skirving, a farmer and former divinity student who left a wife and large family. The five became known, and celebrated, as the Scottish Martyrs, though interestingly only two, Muir and Skirving, were in fact Scottish.

As the public mood darkened further Robert Burns's fear turned to alarm. He lamented that it was not possible to make the slightest criticism of the Government, or even pass a remark in a pub, without being accused of sedition. In Dumfries middle class acquaintances cut him dead in the street, and even Mrs. Dunlop, his friend and confidante, cut off correspondence. In his distress he wrote:-

> The shrinking Bard adown an alley skulks,
> And dreads a meeting worse than Woolwich hulks
> – Tho' there his heresies in Church and State
> Might well award him Muir and Palmer's fate. (3)

The Woolwich hulks he refers to were the prison ships on which Muir and the other martyrs were held before transportation.

For Thomas Muir, the events that followed have all the elements of an exaggerated adventure story. After sixteen months in the colony he made a dramatic escape on an American trading ship, *The Otter*.

He then faced many stirring encounters with the South Sea Islanders and the Red Indians of Nootka Sound on the West Coast of America, sometimes greeted with hospitality and other times with life threatening hostility. His treatment by the Spanish in Mexico veered between that of a guest and a prisoner. Then on his return to Europe the Spanish ship he was on was attacked by the British off Trafalgar. Muir was struck by a cannon ball, casing him to lose his left eye and suffer serious facial disfigurement.

Taken prisoner by the British, they failed to recognise their prisoner, as he hovered on the brink of death. But then amidst his dire misfortune he had a miraculous stroke of good luck. Through the inscription on his Bible he was recognised by a British surgeon who had been a student with Muir at Glasgow University. Instead of informing the British authorities he treated his injuries as best he could and tipped-off the Spanish. Through the diplomatic intersession of the French government Muir was eventually returned to France where he was regaled as a hero of liberty. There he joined Thomas Paine, Wolfe Tone of the United Irishmen and other political exiles. However, he never recovered from his injuries and died on 26th January 1799. He was only 33 years old.

Thomas Muir's place in history rests not on what he achieved but in what he began, and the inspiration and guidance he imparted to succeeding generations of reformers. When the great Reform Act of 1832 was achieved it was Muir and the other Scottish martyrs who were lionised in Kilsyth and throughout Britain. Kilsyth weaver, John Kirkwood did so by a satirical attack on Gilbert Innes of Stow, the wealthy foreman of the jury that convicted Muir.

> He showed, when born to the regions of night,
> Such knowledge of matters infernal,
> That the Devil himself, at very first sight,
> Made him Prince of a province eternal!

> But Satan remembered his partner in power,
> That he, while on earth, was a traitor.
> That is tenderest feelings were prone to devour –
> That he was a demon by nature.

So, deeming it prudent to have him deposed,
And anxious to hasten his fall;
Yet the fire of his fury was never disclosed
'Till he kicked him out over the wall!

And whether he will yet return to the earth
Is more than we mortals will know;
But one thing is certain, that e'er since his birth
He proved himself Liberty's foe.

So perish all such from the visible world!
Is the prayer of All – save the ninnies,
Who shortly shall feel what it is to be hurl'd
From their stations, like poor Gilbert Innes.

(Kilsyth, 1st May 1832) (4)

Thomas Muir may have also been written out of the history books but they could not erase his memory from the minds and hearts of the people. Throughout the campaigns and battles of the nineteenth century when our democracy was forged, Muir was the bedrock and inspiration through troubled times. In September 1844 a ninety foot high monument to the memory of the 'Five Scottish Martyrs' was erected after £900 was raised at events throughout Britain. It still stands on the old burial ground at Calton Hill in Edinburgh – erected by 'The Friends of Parliamentary Reform in England and Scotland'.

(1) Bewley, Christina *Muir of Huntershill – A Scottish patriot's Adventures around the world* Oxford University Press
(2) Calney, Mark *Robert Burns and the Ideas of the American Revolution*
(3) McIlvanney, Liam *Burns the Radical* (Tuckwell Press)
(4) *The Reformers Gazette* (p357)

CHAPTER 6

THE REV. JOHN ANDERSON was ordained at the Kilsyth Relief Church on September 12th 1793, only two weeks after the trial of Thomas Muir, and on the same day as the Rev. Thomas Fyshe Palmer was tried at Perth and also sentenced to transportation to Australia. John Anderson was no disinterested observer of these events.

In such tumultuous times the 22 year-old began his 69 year ministry at Kilsyth. His son Robert was to succeed him, and the Anderson dynasty lasted over one hundred years. If its longevity was unique, so too was the quality and nature of the service rendered. He chose Kilsyth despite having two other offers from parishes with stipends twenty-five per cent higher, no small factor for a man who was to have 14 children – five sons and two daughters by his first wife (Margaret Watt) and then a repeat five sons and two daughters by his second wife (Jean Muir) The only explanation he offered for his choice of Kilsyth was at his jubilee in 1843. 'It was from heaven I think I preferred your fathers and you,' he said.

The Anderson family arose from a different part of the social compass than Thomas Muir. Old William, John's father, was an early product of the dawning industrial revolution. He began his working life as a joiner with the new Carron Iron Company. He became fascinated by the first pumping engine in Scotland which kept the Carron Dam (a pond adjacent to the works) supplied with water from the river. In his spare time he studied the engine and became proficient in its workings. He went on to invent the automatic ball-cock valve to self-regulate the supply of water to the boiler, which remains in use today in boilers and cisterns.

William prospered and was able to buy a small farm near Airth. His future seemed assured but then came a crisis which put everything in jeopardy. Anderson was a deeply committed and principled

Calvinist of the old school. His grandson tells of how 'late one Sabbath night something went wrong with the engine. Set right it must be, or there would be a stoppage of work at Carron on Monday morning. A messenger on horseback arrived at my grandfather's door, telling him to come at once and sort the engine. For him to work on the Sabbath was impossible, for conscience sake. He sent the messenger away to tell Mr. Stanton that he would be at Carron as soon after twelve as his horse could bring him. He knew what the consequences were likely to be, and told his wife that in all probability his connection with Carron Works was at an end. It was a sore trial to her, and she confessed afterwards how she was tempted to put forward the long hand of the clock. After half past eleven the messenger returned with a led horse, but the stubborn man was immovable, and again he had to go away.

'Twelve o'clock struck at last. Only then he saddled his pony and sped swiftly along the road. He was met at Carrongate with a torrent of crashing oaths, and ordered off to the enginehouse. He did not go. He faced Mr. Stanton, and told him that he had a higher Master than the company; that he must, and would, obey the law of God, and that if he could not do this in the company's service he must leave. He then asked Mr. Stanton to tell him whether he was to go or remain.'

'Away,' said Stanton 'and set the engine agoing.' But William Anderson still lingered.

'I am deeply grieved,' he said, 'that you should have made me the cause of such awful blasphemy.'

'Anderson,' said Mr. Stanton, 'I have been hasty, too hasty; away and set things right and no more about it.' And so the incident passed. When asked later why he did not dismiss Anderson, Mr. Stenton's reply, as reported, was to the effect, 'I knew his worth, and felt that if, at such risk, he could be true to his God, he would be true to me.'

Old William was an elder in the Relief Church at Falkirk until his death in his eighties. We now know the source of that courageous and unyielding adherence to principle which was to manifest itself in the Andersons that followed. It was not for them to wrap up the spiritual and temporal lives in neat separate packages, and be content to preach charity to the rich and resignation to the poor.

The health and progress of the 'Godly Commonwealth' of

Presbyterian doctrine was their concern and duty. This was the source of what was described as John Anderson's 'advanced political creed.'

The young John Anderson was educated at Edinburgh and Glasgow universities, and proved a brilliant student becoming an authority in English literature and the classics. His scholastic achievements were all the more remarkable in that he took his degree when merely a boy.

It was in Edinburgh that he had his first clash with the civic powers. His grandson Robert related, 'that while my father was yet a mere boy and attending classes in Edinburgh he narrowly escaped imprisonment in the Heart of Midlothian,' the jail of Sir Walter Scott's story of the Porteous Riots. Robert Anderson relates how his father 'attended a secret political meeting, presided over by Lord Daer. The doors were forced by the military, and those who could, of whom my father was one, escaped in the confusion. Those who did not were lodged in the damp prison cells.'

Lord Daer, who organised the illegal meeting was only six years older than Anderson and was to become one of the most prominent, if unusual leaders of the Reform movement. He belonged to one of Scotland's highest aristocratic families being the eldest surviving son and heir of the Earl of Selkirk, but he was deeply committed to democratic reform; a fervent supporter of the French Revolution and a close associate of Thomas Muir and founder member of the Scottish Society of the Friends of the People. He was the first aristocrat that Robert Burns met socially. Despite Burns previous scathing denunciations of the aristocracy he was invited to dinner with Lord Daer by Professor Dugald Stewart of the Chair of Moral Philosophy at Edinburgh University, at his home, Catrine Bank near Mauchline. Burns was so impressed by the young aristocrat that he composed a poem in his honour. It concluded,

> Then from his Lordship I shall learn,
> Henceforth to meet with unconcern
> One rank as weel's another;
> Nae honest, worthy man need care
> To meet with noble youthful Daer.
> For he but meets a brother.

Great hopes were rested on Lord Daer's future but his health was always fragile and sadly he died prematurely in France in 1794.

John Anderson's second known clash with the State came when he was a young minister in Kilsyth. It took place even before his ordination when he was a stand-in at the Relief Church. Robert Anderson relates,

> 'The country was over-run with Government spies. No Kilsyth man was ever suspected of belonging to the hated brotherhood, but all visitors to the town were dangerous, whether clad in moleskin or broadcloth. A plausible gentleman, full of curiosity about the Battle of Kilsyth, and who had travelled all the way from England to identify its locality in the interests of accurate history, nearly entrapped my father. He introduced politics into the conversation in a way that excited timely suspicion. He turned up next day in Kirkintilloch and succeeded better with the Rev. William Dunn, who, for his half-hour's entertainment of his guest and his expression of sympathy with his people, suffered some months imprisonment in the county jail.'

However, there was much more to the story than that. The Rev. William Dunn was no naive country minister but a close friend and confidant of Thomas Muir, and he was not jailed for making indiscreet comments in support of his people but for destroying evidence the Crown was seeking in their pursuit of Muir. What is more, John Anderson played a bigger role in the drama than is suggested as he was cited as a witness at Dunn's trial but was not called due to a legal technicality.

Indeed, the prosecution of William Dunn sheds light on the larger national drama, namely how the net of repression was closing on the reformers. The first branches of the Friends of the People were formed in Edinburgh, led by prominent progressive Whig lawyers, Lord Daer and others close to the Edinburgh establishment. This development gave the Government concern but what then happened in Glasgow alarmed them.

On 3rd of October 1792 knots of weavers and other working men assembled outside the Star Inn at the head of Glassford Street where they were hearing reports and discussing events taking place in France. They then entered the hotel and were addressed by Thomas Muir who was cheered to the rafters. The meeting then decided to form a branch of the Friends of the People. It made no difference that each member had to sign a declaration expressing loyalty to the Crown, and that he was of good moral character. From that moment when Thomas Muir involved working people in the battle for democracy he was targeted as Public Enemy Number One.

Only six days after the Star Hotel meeting the Rev. William Dunn, who had been elected to serve a period as moderator of the Synod of Glasgow and Ayr, delivered the traditional sermon at the Old Tron, only a few hundred yards from the Star Hotel.

Even reading the sermon today, it is an impressive and eloquent plea for reform in government, the arts and religious institutions. As described at the time, it had 'sprinklings of lofty liberality about it'. It concluded by exhorting the people 'to be enemies of riot and sedition, unintimidated by difficulties, and incapable of forgetting your birth-right as Britons – love your God, honour your King, venerate the constitution, maintain the laws of your country.' He went on to say, 'Contribute your part to make all Europe sensible that the profligate opinion is no longer to be received – that the people are made for the prince, and not the prince for and by the people; that nations are no longer to be sacrificed to the vanity of princes, and the rapacity of those about them.' (1)

The lay members of the Synod were so impressed they decided to have the sermon published at their own expense. The clergy, who owed their position to patronage, were more reticent. William Dunn, however, could never have dreamt that his celebrated sermon would set running a series of events that would lead him to a prison cell.

Some fanciful accounts were written about what followed, but from official papers and other sources we can construct a credible account of what happened. On Friday 4th January 1793, less than three months after delivery of the sermon, Sir James Colquhoun, the Sheriff Depute of Dunbartonshire, and his posse rode into Kirkintilloch. He was there on the instructions of none other than the Lord Advocate Robert

Dundas who claimed that he had information that a Society of Reform set up there had been guilty of seditious proceedings, and that the minutes of the Society's meetings contained treasonable matters and correspondence. The Sheriff questioned several witnesses at a local hotel, including James Baird, secretary of the Society, who admitted he had the Society's minutes book. It was a 'difficult' interrogation for Baird who was clearly playing for time. Eventually, he agreed to go to his home and retrieve the book. Excusing his delay in returning he said the book, which had been at his home that morning, had been removed. However, he eventually had found it at the home of local innkeeper William Wallace.

It was immediately detected that three pages of the book had been ripped out. Without hesitation Baird explained that they had been destroyed by the Rev. William Dunn, who was immediately summoned before the Sheriff. Dunn frankly confirmed Baird's account in full, a clear indication that there had been collusion. He admitted burning the pages. He said he was visiting a parishioner, Mrs. Oswald, and while at tea John Scott and two others arrived. They told him the sheriff was carrying out an investigation in the town and they asked him to look over a book which was titled *The Reform Society of Kirkitilloch*. He had no objection in doing so but when he read references in praise of a sermon he had delivered to the Synod, he panicked. He ripped out the three leaves referring to him, went upstairs to the room where he had been having tea and cast them in the fire. He admitted to having acted rashly and impulsively. The law officers concluded, probably correctly, that more than references to the minister's sermon had been consigned to the flames.

It may have been that the books of the society were secreted at the home of Mrs. Oswald in anticipation of a raid by the authorities. Certainly, in Dunn's defence statement, care was taken to exonerate her from any involvement.

The first question that arises is why did the Lord Advocate, Robert Dundas, order a seizure of the Kirkintilloch Reform Society's books? It should be borne in mind that at that time the Crown was desperately trying to build a case of sedition or treason against Thomas Muir. Despite the fact that Muir had addressed literally hundreds of meetings, many of them infiltrated by spies, they could not find a single instance of him making any statement which was unlawful or advocating unlawful activity. The Crown had obviously been informed that at the meeting of the Kirkintilloch Reform Society, which Muir had attended and addressed, comments or actions were made or taken which would sustain a prosecution against Muir. In the legal papers there is a clue to what that information referred to.

The reformers of Paisley had issued a document which became known as the 'Paisley Declaration' which was regarded as both seditious and treasonable, and we know a copy had been sent to Muir. We also know that the *Kirkintilloch Society* had copies of the Declaration although there was no evidence that it was Muir who supplied them.

Although Muir played no part in compiling the Declaration if he were even to refer to its contents, or participate in a discussion about it, that would be taken as evidence that could sustain a prosecution. It is interesting to note that when summoned before the Sheriff, Dunn was questioned on the Declaration. He replied that 'he never saw the Paisley Declaration of Rights, until it was now shown to him; and that Mr. Thomas Muir, never showed the declarant any political papers,' a clear indication that the Declaration was at the forefront of the investigation. The evidence clearly indicates that it was Muir, the Crown was pursuing, and that they had no interest in Dunn until he put himself in the frame by burning the pages.

Later at Muir's trial the Crown again made strenuous but unsuccessful efforts to associate Muir with the Declaration.

The question then arises: in whose interests was William Dunn acting when he exposed himself to prosecution by burning the pages in the book? Certainly not his own. He claimed he panicked when he saw his name in reference to the celebrated sermon he had delivered to the Synod. The Crown did not believe him, and with good cause. After all, had the Sheriff questioned him about it, he had a cast-iron defence. He was not a member of the Reform Society and did not attend any of its meetings. All he knew was what he was told, that a vote of thanks had been passed at a meeting in regard to his sermon, which he neither invited or had any control over. Besides, there was nothing in the sermon to apologise for. Not only had it been widely publicised and celebrated, but had been published as a pamphlet by the members of a Synod of the Church of Scotland itself. Who then was William Dunn protecting in what he described as his 'harsh act'?

One obvious figure was his close friend Thomas Muir. We do not know what was said or done at the Reform Society meeting, if anything, but Dunn either knew or suspected that contents of the book could incriminate Muir by association. He would also be aware of the danger to his friends and parishioners in the Reform Society. If the Government was prepared to cast an ordained minister of the Church of Scotland into prison, what would they do to working class radicals who deliberately destroyed a whole body of evidence?

The known facts point to a damage limitation plan quickly concocted by Dunn himself in conversation with the Reform Society officials at the home of Mrs. Oswald. To protect the officials they could not withhold the book, yet, they were anxious not to allow the Crown access to certain contents. The plan met these objectives, but at the cost of placing William Dunn in the firing line.

He maintained his story, and when taken to the High Court pleaded for clemency. The three judges who tried him were also not impressed with his account, but probably mindful of public reaction and the lack of concrete evidence, they confined his sentence to three months in the notorious Tolbooth of Edinburgh. They added sourly that had he been served with an indictment rather than a petition, they would 'have inflicted on him the highest arbitrary punishment'. If there was any doubt that it was Muir and not Dunn who was their target, it was made clear in the Crown's case when they alleged that Dunn had received letters from Thomas Muir that he could not produce. Dunn replied that the letters were of inconsequential matters and he had no reason to retain them. (2)

It appears beyond doubt the Rev. William Dunn's part in the affair was an extraordinary act of self sacrifice to protect his friends. When released from prison his parishioners and supporters crowded the Kilsyth Road to welcome him home. A woman who knew the minister well in her girlhood days told Robert Anderson 'of his wrongs, the anger of the crowd, and the increased respect and love which he received when returned to liberty.'

The part played by John Anderson in the affair remains shrouded in mystery, as does all his political activity, for Anderson was the heart and soul of discretion. What is known is that he knew well and communicated with many of the national reform leaders of the time. He was particularly friendly with Thomas Muir who he first befriended when they were at university together. Indeed, his second wife, Jean Muir, Robert Anderson's mother, was a first cousin of Thomas Muir. Robert is somewhat coy about the family relationship but he did write,

> 'I have heard my mother tell how, when she was a girl, living at Birdston, in the parish of Campsie, Mr. Muir of Huntershill, a young man of birth and scholarship, used to come and address secret meetings in a barn in that quiet clachan. His politics, which were but the alphabet of things as they are now, cost him his country, for the ruling powers of the day banished him across the seas.'

However, the Dunn affair was not to be the last time that Government agents were to take an interest in the activities of the young radical Kilsyth minister. It was amidst such stirring events his long and distinguished ministry began. On his commitment to social reform it was said in his funeral oration that 'he lived to see proscribed opinions triumph, and rejoiced as he saw the strongholds of Toryism stormed one after another, and monopoly after monopoly broken up, and an amount of liberty enjoyed by his fellow countrymen greater than that of any other people on the face of the globe.'

---

(1) Sermon preached at opening of Synod of Glasgow and Ayr:, 9th October 1792 by Rev. William Dunn. (National Library of Scotland MF.134,reel 13371)
(2) Dunn (Rev.) William: Petition of Lord Advocate: National Library of Scotland L.C. 1133:ESTC T217386

CHAPTER 7

Why did those seceding and protesting ministers such as John Anderson and William Dunn, who were amongst the brightest and most altruistic of the age, pit themselves against an all powerful State at such great personal cost and danger to them and their families? The first point to make is their political and social stand was not something apart from their religious ministry but central to it. They may have arrived at similar commitments to extending human and civil rights for all people, and democracy as a means of achieving that end, but they got there from quite a different direction than secular campaigners.

In fact we have to go right back to a tension, some would say a contradiction, which lay at the heart of Calvinism and its doctrine of predestination. Calvinism held that at the dawn of time God chose a lucky few called the Elect to be saved. The rest would be damned and cast into hell no matter what they did. The terrible problem for Calvinists was how they could know if they were of the Elect or the damned. In the world of work they found an answer to this agonising spiritual predicament. Success in the every day material world was regarded as a sign from God that they were members of the Elect, marked out for salvation.

The Protestant work ethic was born and the link between spiritual and private capital was forged. Wealth was the best evidence of God's favour. But there was another side to Calvinist doctrine which some chose to ignore. The purpose of work and wealth accumulation was to glorify God, not to achieve personal riches. Calvin believed in just and responsible economic activity within the confines of a Godly Commonwealth. Money making was only acceptable if it went hand in hand with Christian morals.

Calvin was only too well aware of the corrupting influence of wealth and wealth-seeking for non-religious purposes, and he went into minute detail of what was and what was not acceptable. 'No member of the Christian body,' he wrote in his *Institutes of Christianity* holds his gifts to himself, for his private use, but shares them among his fellow members, nor does he derive benefit save from those things which proceed from the common profit of the body as a whole. Thus the pious man owes to his brethren all that is in his power to give.' (1)

On the one hand Calvinism sanctified individualism, work and profit making, and was said to have released, or at least legitimised, the spirit of capitalism. On the other hand there was the ethical conscience of Protestantism which rested on the doctrine of the 'priesthood of all believers', a conviction that all men stood equal before the judgment of God within a Godly Commonwealth.

Protestant-inspired capitalism and the Protestant social conscience have been in conflict for the last five centuries in some of the most contentious issues in history. (2) It goes some way to explain why Christians of the same faith were amongst the most cruel and barbaric slave traders while fellow Christians not only opposed slavery but led the battle against it in the first global civil rights movement in history. It also goes some way to explain how the Ku Klux Klan and the civil rights campaigners of Dr. Martin Luther King could claim the same Christian heritage and faith.

The clash over slavery, more than any other issue, ripped open the contradiction that lay at the heart of Protestant thought. Twelve million Africans were seized from their homelands and taken as slaves to the New World. Three million died in indescribable horror during transportation. The issue pitted the value systems of Protestantism against each other and the Bible was scoured to justify the trade in human life. The ethical conscience wing of the Church regarded the trade as a monstrous breach of the Calvinist idea of the Godly Commonwealth as was possible to imagine. The fierce anti-slavery campaign was largely waged by the nonconformist churches in England, such as the Methodists, and the Seceding churches in Scotland. The Methodists even took the battle to Barbados, the slavery capital of the British Empire. For their trouble they were driven from the island by their Anglican fellow Christians and their churches burned to the ground.

The Abolitionists, however, eventually triumphed and in 1806 slave trading was abolished in the British Empire. But abolition of slave trading did not bring closure to the conflict. There was the question of thousands of slaves who had been taken into captivity and the issue of compensation, not for the slaves but for the slave owners' loss of property.

Robert Anderson recalls as a schoolboy at the time, many lively public meetings in Kilsyth on the issue. One ended in uproar. The radicals headed by Dr. Wallace and Tom Ney said,

> 'the slaves of commerce at home were worse off than the black ones they had been hearing about, for although when lazy, the latter had to work under the lash, they were cared for in housing and food; but the home slaves of trade, whether lazy or not, had to work from morning till night under the whip of poverty, double thonged with cold and hunger, and with wife and children crying to them for bread. It would be more like the thing to distribute the twenty million pounds among the starving workmen than among these slaveholders of the West Indies.'

In the end the slave owners got their twenty million pounds from the British Government but interestingly the Kilsyth radicals had anticipated the next battle ground in the progressive agenda. The resolution of slavery did not end the struggle for the soul of Presbyterianism. It just moved on to new grounds closer to home. Indeed, there is the view that one reason slavery was ended was because it had become uneconomic. With the growth of the poor and downtrodden of Europe flooding into the New World it became cheaper to hire and fire than keep slaves.

The Scots-born Irish socialist James Connolly made the point in relating this incident:

> 'A negro slave in the southern States of America was told by his owner to go up and fasten the shingles on top of the roof of his

master's dwelling. 'Boss,' said he to the slave-owner, 'if I go up there and fall down and get killed you will lose that 500 dollars you paid for me; but if you send up that Irish labourer and he falls down and breaks his neck you won't even have to bury him, and can get another labourer tomorrow for two dollars a day.' The Irish labourer was sent up. The Moral: Slavery is immoral because slaves cost too much.'

Certainly, following emancipation little changed. The plantation workers continued to work for starvation wages and in appalling conditions. But their status had changed if not their daily lives. They joined the new category of wage slaves that stretched all the way back to Britain.

By now the Industrial Revolution was well underway and was driven by red in tooth and claw capitalism. Pursuit of profit was not just the first priority but the only one as the dark Satanic mills of Blake's poem sprang up with the brutal exploitation and degradation of men, women and children on a horrendous scale. Indeed, the slave owners often argued, and with some justification, that the slave in the cotton field was better off than the worker in the cotton mills back home. Cheap badly built houses were thrown-up for the new factory workers who were crowded into the slums, sometimes nine to a room. One doctor told how these living and working conditions produced a small, sick and degenerate race, human beings stunted, enfeebled and depraved.

As the industrial revolution gained pace through the 1800s, the coal miners and mill workers particularly shared these lamentable conditions. In the mills children as young as five, named 'nippies', leapt between the looms at great risk, and when a little older they worked fourteen hours a day in the most dangerous and damaging conditions. These industrial hells were a terrible culmination of the Protestant work ethic. Once again the excesses of capitalism called into question the values at the heart of Protestantism. But the opposition exploded within the Church as Christians joined with others in a national campaign against the new industrial order. They eventually won a Parliamentary inquiry into working conditions in

Britain, and its findings shocked the conscience of the country.

One witness, Elisa Marshall, told how she began working in a textile factory at the age of nine. When she first went to the mill she worked from six in the morning to seven in the evening. After a time she began at five in the morning and worked till ten at night. She was often beaten when younger, and had an iron on her deformed leg caused by standing for hours on end. The nineteenth century was to be a long battle for industrial reform.

The new industrial order was just taking off when John Anderson took office in Kilsyth in 1793, and the young minister found he had urgent pastoral concerns to address. According to his grandson, Robert Anderson there were not more than half-a-dozen of those who sat at his father's first communion who were not, more or less, avowed sceptics.

> 'Things went far. The Bible was even, by some of the bolder of the infidels in the town, made a bonfire of up in the Glen, at the 'Deil's Seat', who, no doubt, was there at the time. This state of things gave character to my father's preaching. Each sermon was a theological treatise, clear in statement, and reasoned out to its conclusions. It was not time for literary ornamentation and rhetorical flourishes. He had to prove all things, and hold fast that which was good. In this he was not alone. All over the country ministers were beset by the same influences as he, and had to encounter them in the same way. The pulpits of Scotland in the early part of the century were filled by intellectual athletes, who vindicated truth on the arena of pure reason, and the moral sense of men.'

The cause of this 'tide of infidelity' in his view was the French Revolution, which was 'atheistic and immoral, abjuring Christianity and Christians. . .

> 'It might have been thought that a Christian community would have turned away from it with horror. My father did not find so. There was the political side to the French uprising, and it

> appealed to the feelings and passion of the people so strongly, as
> to make the most of them more than tolerant of its antagonism
> to religion. They were fed too with infidel literature. Voltaire
> was but fifteen years dead, and his writings were scattered
> broadcast over the land. It was in 1793 that Tom Paine
> published his 'Rights of Man'. These books had then all the
> charm of novelty and the force of a keen wit. The book-reading
> weavers of Kilsyth devoured them all at their firesides,
> discussed them at the street corners, and through their political
> sympathies sucked in their poison.'

Robert Anderson somewhat overstates his case, though we must
remember he was writing of these events the best part of a century
later and compressing a lot of material and events. In the first place
Voltaire and Paine were not atheists at all – they were Deists; and
Tom Paine's onslaught on revealed religion, *The Age of Reason*, was
not published until several years after the period under consideration.
The Rights of Man, to which he referred contained no anti-religious
theme. Indeed, Paine stated in that book: 'Every religion is good that
teaches man to be good; and I know of none that teaches him to be
bad.' (3)

Ironically, what moved Paine to write *The Age of Reason* was that
he shared the dismay of Christians over the lapse of the Revolution
into atheism and secularism. He foresaw the dangers of descending
into 'the false systems of government and theology and losing sight
of morality, humanity and of the theology that is true.' (4)

It should be noted that the Kilsyth weavers did not withdraw
from the Kirk. Even according to Robert Anderson's account they
were sceptical but remained in the congregation. Surely their
scepticism could be justified both in terms of the principles of
Calvinism and the Enlightenment which held that every belief should
be tested against Scripture and every conviction subject to the tests of
reason and evidence. It could be reasonably argued that such
fundamental soul-searching from first principles was in the end no
bad thing for the weavers or the Kirk.

As for the 'Devil worship in the Garrell Glen' – if it is not apocryphal the participants could hardly have been representative of the body of weavers. It defies credibility that this body of men who studied and were informed and inspired by the great thinkers of the Enlightenment could possibly have been lured into demonolatry. Besides, the weavers did not have to go far from home to find sceptical arguments. David Hume, the greatest philosopher of the age, was a Scot and an avowed atheist. It was fortunate for him that he was not born a few years earlier. Only fourteen years before his birth in 1711 Thomas Aikenhead, like Hume a student at Edinburgh University, became the last person in Britain to be executed for blasphemy. The young student's crime was to question and refute the basic tenets of Christianity. The clinching evidence was that on his way home with friends one cold winter night he said, 'I wish I were in that place called Hell so I could warm myself.'

He was locked-up in the Tolbooth and brought before the High Court. He attempted to recant his views and made a plea for mercy. But mercy was in short supply and he was sentenced to be taken to the gallows between Edinburgh and Leith and that he be hanged and his body buried under the gallows.

Petitions for clemency were made on his behalf. The Church of Scotland's General Assembly was meeting in the city at that time and could have saved him but they urged 'vigorous execution' to curb 'the abounding impiety and profanity in this land.' Such tyranny always sows the seeds of its own destruction.

Although David Hume was to face victimisation, and the greatest philosopher of the age was to be denied a professorship, no attempts were made to bring the full power of the criminal law against him, as over that relatively short time the authority of the fanatics had waned.

---

(1) Tawney R.H. *The Rise of Capitalism*
(2) Tristam Hunt *The Protestant Revolution*
(3) Paine Thomas *The Rights of Man*
(4) Thomas Paine *The Age of Reason*

CHAPTER 8

IN THOSE EARLY YEARS of the Anderson dynasty the people had more elemental concerns. The periodic slumps in trade were more than a minor irritation, but when work shortage combined with a drastic harvest, as happened in 1801, the spectre of famine stalked the land. John Anderson never spoke of that year but with bated breath. Looms were idle, the corn rotted in the stook 'as famine entered the homes of God's people'. It was a woe-stricken Kilsyth that year 'of gaunt men and women, and white-cheeked children. Meal rose to 4s.6d. a peck. Even the few who had money had difficulty getting it at that inflated price, though they besieged the farmhouses as far apart as Glasgow and Stirling.' John Anderson spent the money he had as he set the suffering weavers to work building a boundary dyke around the manse garden.

It was hard enough to endure when these conditions were caused by natural catastrophe but they were to become the outcome of deliberate Government policy, namely the Corn Laws, which were to cause bitter and enduring resentment. The Corn Laws were designed to protect the profits of the aristocratic landowners who controlled the economy and the Government. The laws imposed a duty on imported grain until they reached a price that would safeguard the landowners profit levels. The first Corn Law was enacted in 1804 and then strengthened with a vengeance at the end of the Napoleonic War in 1815. Protests erupted throughout the country and Parliament had to be defended by armed troops. For the weavers the Corn Laws had a double jeopardy – their goods were banned from foreign ports in retaliation causing widespread unemployment while the cost of bread, their staple diet rose to levels beyond their means.

Early on the Kilsyth weavers made their protest. They met in the

Relief Church and decided to petition Parliament. The petition, written personally by John Anderson, put their case.

'To the Honourable, the Commons of Great Britain and Ireland in Parliament assembled.

'The petition of the inhabitants of Kilsyth, Stirlingshire, humbly showeth that the great majority of your petitioners, with many thousands of their fellow subjects, are in a state of great suffering from the failure of trade and commerce; that the number of poor and destitute has increased, and is increasing to a deplorable extent; and that without a change in the measures of the national government, they can not only have no hope of a favourable turn but have cause to dread some public convulsion. Also, whatever influence other causes may have had in producing this state of affairs, the Corn and Provision Laws stand prominently forward as causing them; that these laws are cruel, unworthy of you honourable House, and grossly impolitic, as shutting foreign ports against our manufactured goods, and forcing the best of our artisans from their native homes. In the hope that your honourable House will lend an ear to the groanings of suffering humanity, and save your country from threatened ruin, we earnestly entreat you to repeal the Corn and Provision Laws, and allow your petitioners and all others to purchase food where it may be found cheapest and best. And your petitioners will ever pray. . . etc'

Needless to say the petition along with hundreds of others was ignored. The battle was to continue for decades until the Corn Laws were finally abolished in 1846. As late as 1842 Friedrich Engels rightly predicted that though the English nobility had reluctantly accepted the 1832 Reform Act, 'this time I am firmly convinced they will remain adamant until the knife is at their throat.'

Hatred of the Corn Laws were to inform and fuel every disturbance and protest by the people throughout half that troubled century, from the Peterloo Massacre, to the Scottish Insurrection of 1820 to the campaign for the great Reform Act of 1832.

The Corn Laws controversy may at first sight appear as an obscure issue from a bygone age but in fact the issue at its heart resonates today. The weavers would have been deeply conscious of the hypocrisy and double-standards being applied. When the weavers pleaded for government intervention to bring some degree of stability to their trade and their lives they were solemnly told it was not possible as any interference with the invisible hand of the market would lead to grave and unforeseen perils. But it turned out that the sanctity of the market depended on whose interests were at stake. When the profits of the landed aristocracy were threatened the laws of the market were swiftly set aside. The weavers were not the last to confront this contradiction.

But what had happened to the Reform Movement? By the closing months of 1793 the Friends of the People appeared to be comprehensively crushed. Muir and the other leaders had been transported, and the Government was confident enough to be even more repressive. On top of that, given the flight of the middle class from the field of battle and the divisions opened up by the imperial advances of France, it appeared that the campaign for democracy was over. However, there was to be one further desperate effort to save the day.

Two Edinburgh reformers, Robert Watt, a former Government spy turned Radical, and David Downie, decided to abandon constitutional means and planned a Scottish insurrection to begin in Edinburgh. They formed a Ways and Means committee, ostensibly to collect funds for the families of the Scottish Martyrs but in fact the money was to be used for the 'great cause'. The audacious plan was to seize Edinburgh Castle, the Post Office, the banks and the Excise Office. At the same time a number of prominent people would be targeted for arrest, including the Lords of Judiciary, the Magistrates and the Lord Provost of Edinburgh. At the beginning of May 1794 Watt sent an emissary, John Fairly, to visit the leading radical centres in the West of Scotland. He had to deliver a set of papers which hinted at the insurrection plan and contained instructions on how money and weapons were to be collected and dispatched. The rallying call stated:

'Citizens, there is but one thing that can rescue us, a complete
reform in parliament. Let us not be awed into a servile
submission by any illegal artifice; let us not sink beneath the
beast of oppression; but let us unite firmer than ever. . . never
let us relinquish this great work.' (1)

Fairly had also to assess the measure of support in the centres he
visited. The only recorded response was from Stirling who pledged to
supply funding but nothing beyond that. What happened following
his visit to Stirling was related by Fairly when giving evidence at the
trial of David Downie. The Lord Advocate questioned him on his
visit to Stirling and then asked, 'Where did you go then?
Fairly: 'To Kilsyth'
Lord Advocate: 'Whom did you see there?'
Fairly: 'Mr. Anderson and Mr. Yule. Mr. Anderson is a minister and
    Mr. Yule is a minister.'
Lord Advocate: 'Where did you see them?'
Fairly: 'I took them to Mr. Anderson, and he took them to Mr.
    Yule.'
Lord Advocate: 'Did you leave the papers with them?'
Fairly: 'Yes.'
Lord Advocate: 'Where next?'
Fairly: 'To Campsie. Mr. Yule went with me.' (2)
Fairly then related how he went on to deliver papers in
Kirkintilloch, Glasgow and Paisley. John Anderson would not have
known about the plan far less approve of it. The probability is that
Fairly was directed to him because he was the only supporter of reform
in the area known by name in Edinburgh. It is not known who Mr.
Yule was but there is a reference to a Charles Yule as a contact in
Kilsyth.

But shortly after Fairly's return to Edinburgh the plot was
betrayed. Watt and Downie were arrested and charged with High
Treason. They were sentenced to be hanged, drawn and quartered.
Robert Watt duly was executed and Downie had his sentence
commuted to banishment from the country.

In the National Museum of Scotland there are two Pike-Heads

made for that armed struggle which were recovered in Kilsyth. It is known they were donated to the Museum in 1841 by a Miss Wilson from Kilsyth. But, intriguingly, their label states 'Pike-Heads – Friends of the People, Kilsyth.' (3)

We know the Friends of the People was a non-violent organisation. By the time they had drawn up their plans the Friends of the People had all but collapsed following the transportation of Muir and the other leaders. It is unlikely, however, that the authorities would distinguish between the organisation and Watt and Downie, who had been members of the Friends of the People. It is also worthy of note that when John Fairly visited Kilsyth and other radical centres he not only appealed for arms but provided a detailed blueprint for the design of pikes. The Kilsyth Pike-Heads closely resemble other surviving Pike-Heads seized in Edinburgh which were said to have been made by Robert Orrock, an Edinburgh blacksmith.

However, by now the Reform movement appeared dead and buried. Robert Anderson claimed that as the conflict with France loomed 'all minor causes of social discord, all political unrest ceased in the presence of that danger. The Radicals were all patriots, and this was not the time to discuss their rights and wrongs, not till this French business was seen and settled.'

This sentiment was no doubt abroad but it is far from being the whole story. The flickering flame of democracy was not extinguished. It was kept alive, not so much in the pubs and salons of Edinburgh but in rural weaving communities such as Kilsyth. Local reform groups continued to form and meet in communities throughout Scotland.

Gradually and long before 1797 when the Government learned of its existence, the local reform groups had formed into a new national body, The United Scotsmen, which derived its name from the United Irishmen, with which it was in close consort. The Government would be less surprised to learn that a branch, or branches, of this new body had been set-up and were active in Kilsyth. (4)

The United Scotsmen was different in character and form from its predecessor being exclusively working class, mostly weavers, and more republican and revolutionary in its sympathies. By necessity it went underground as they were well aware that a Government which was only too willing to transport eminent lawyers and clergymen would be even more barbaric in their treatment of those who they contemptuously referred to as the 'lower orders'. New members were inducted by means of a secret oath, and secret handshakes and passwords were used to greet each other. The oath sworn by all members stated:

> 'In the awful presence of God I do voluntary declare, that I will persevere in endeavouring to form a brotherhood of affection amongst Britons of every description; and that I will also persevere in my endeavours to obtain an equal, full, and adequate Representation of all the People in Great Britain. I do further declare, that whatever misfortunes may befall any member or members of this or similar societies, in legally pursuing the objects of this union, I will esteem it my duty to support them lawfully, to the utmost of my ability, so help me God.'

The basic unit was the branch, and when any branch reached sixteen members a new branch was formed in order to limit penetration by Government spies. Interestingly, the United Scotsman was strongest in small rural weaving communities or where there were a large number of church seceders. It had two main centres of activity in Stirlingshire, and it almost goes without saying one of them was Kilsyth.

The stated aims were Universal Suffrage and Annual Parliaments but its longer strategy was to unite with sister organisations in England and Ireland with a view to setting up three republics with the help of the French. There was even a proposal to bring back Thomas Muir to lead a Scottish Government.

Whatever view is taken of this new revolutionary approach one has to admire those intrepid weavers who, despite a daily struggle for survival, and in the face of an unrelenting repressive government, were not prepared to surrender the battle for democracy. If the weavers were now all patriots, as Robert Anderson suggests, their patriotism was being sharply redefined as loyalty to their country and its traditions and values, which were now regarded as quite distinct from support for the governing oligarchy.

We have seen how the cruel Corn Laws accelerated this change, but even the Government was not prepared for the public reaction to their next move – the Militia Act of 1797 – in other words conscription in the army. There had been conscription in England for many years but the Government would not take the risk in Scotland, and for good reason. As one advisor put it, 'It would be rather dangerous to put arms in the hands of the fanatics in the West of Scotland.' By 1797 that risk had to be taken. The threat of foreign invasion was only too real as French privateers began to appear off the Scottish coast.

The new Act ordered the schoolmaster in each parish to make a list of all the able-bodied men between the ages of nineteen and twenty-three. The names were to be posted up at the church door on the Sunday preceding the day fixed for the Deputy-Lieutenants of the district, where complaints were to be heard, the lists revised and a date appointed for a ballot.

Throughout Scotland there were outbursts of fierce resistance. The army was hated by the working class because it was used by the rulers to crush democracy at home and abroad. Disturbances took place in Kilsyth, Kirkintilloch and indeed in towns and villages throughout Scotland. They mostly took the form of local crowds besieging the local headmaster and demanding he hand over the list of candidates for selection. This is what happened in Kilsyth where the parish schoolmaster was threatened, and it was reported that a district meeting was attacked by a crowd consisting 'particularly of manufacturers (weavers) who conducted themselves with great indecency towards the Magistrate.' (5) At Carstairs the local school-house was set ablaze and the fire was only extinguished when the parish registers were given up to the people. But the most dramatic incident, which took the country to the brink of a general uprising, took place at Tranent in East Lothian.

The Depute-Lieutenants, escorted by the local yeomanry and 1,400 English troops of the Pembrokeshire Cavalry, moved into the town to make their selection. They set up office at the local inn which was surrounded by protesters who presented a petition against the

Act which was rejected out of hand. Troops moved in to clear the streets but the protesters reassembled in fields behind the inn and threw stones and anything at hand. The soldiers then opened fire and throwing off all restraint charged across the fields. They continued their mad career for a distance of two miles, shooting or cutting down all who crossed their paths. Eleven people were killed and twelve wounded, most of whom had not taken part in the protest. The incident caused a sensation across the country as the Government refused even to condemn the slaughter far less discipline the soldiers. (6)

As the century drew to a close events conspired against the reformers. There were aborted attempts to land French troops in Ireland and Dutch troops in Scotland. The Scottish population were gradually disheartened by Napoleon's betrayal of the Revolution and his mounting military ambitions. This opened the way for the Government to be even more repressive. Anyone who raised their heads above the parapet faced savage sentences of imprisonment or transportation. The United Scotsmen was declared an illegal organisation and its leaders tried and convicted of seditious activity. They included another weaver, George Mealmaker, who had earlier been a prominent member of the Friends of the People. His crime was to write a pamphlet *The Moral and Political Catechism of Man* which the Crown considered seditious and inflammatory. He was transported to Australia for 14 years, and never returned.

---

(1) Burns, C.M. *Industrial Labour and Radical Movements in Scotland in the 1790s* (M.Sc Thesis. University of Strathclyde 1971)
(2) Thomas James Howell, William Cobbett and David Jardine *Collection of State Trials and Proceedings for High Treason* Vol 24
(3) The National Museum of Scotland (Ref. H.LE680)
(4) O'Neil, Neil McBride *The Progress of Society – Essays on the Scottish Enlightenment*
(5) Ibid
(6) Meikle, H.W. *Scotland And the The French Revolution* (Glasgow 1912)

CHAPTER 9

THE 1812 STRIKE was a momentous watershed in the history of the handloom weavers and their trade with far reaching consequences. Historians now identify it as the end of the Golden Age and the beginning of a century of struggle, hardship and decline. An old weaver in the 1830s looking back put it in more personal terms. He recalled the period before 1812 as 'the daisy portion' of his trade. They built their own houses, ate meat twice a week and were the envy of all trades. Another remembered that then they could 'sit down to a tea breakfast and have their butter and ham like any ordinary furnished table; but the general breakfast now is porridge and buttermilk, and the dinner potatoes and possibly a herring, or any cheap article.'(1)

They may have exaggerated the affluence of the Golden Age, as we know there were times when life was not so golden, but the contrast with the post-strike era was real enough. Yet, Anderson devoted one page to the strike and Anton ignored it completely.

This was Anderson's account:

'In the year 1812 the weaving community became disturbed by agitators, who raised the question of the wrongs of labour at the hands of capitalists. The workers were told they were wronged, robbed and oppressed by the big Glasgow firms for whom they wrought, and it only needed a strike to bring the tyrants to their knees and force them to do right. They did strike. It was the first one in Kilsyth, and was not a success.

'The cheery sound of lay and shuttle ceased in the town, and for weeks the people ate the bread of idleness. They got wild, and went to great excesses. It was a time that tried the prudence of my father and others of influence who had the welfare of the town at heart. A minority was against the strike, and this brought down on them the hot anger of the rest, who gave vent to it in scenes of destructive violence. A strike committee was formed, which fixed a scale of prices at which the manufacturers were to give out webs in Glasgow, and whoever took a web at a less paying rate did so at his peril. Some had webs in the loom when the strike was proclaimed, and because they went on working at them the shop windows were broken, hooked poles were thrust in and the webs torn to pieces, or vitriol was thrown over them. One weaver has told in print how his loomshop was stormed, and that, to appease the angry crowd, he had to 'rump' his web, which means cutting it clean through with a knife. The strikers at last had it their own way, and no one dare move a treadle. After a while, poverty and hunger set in, and the strike ended in misery, leaving behind it harassing debts that could not be paid, and broken friendships that were never healed. What was bitterest of all, the strikers were thankful to get work again at the old prices.' (2)

Whatever his sources, Robert Anderson does less than justice to the striking weavers. To put it down to a few agitators enflaming a gullible community is to ignore the fact that 40,000 weavers across Scotland joined the strike. It was claimed that 'from the German Ocean (the North Sea) to the Irish channel no cotton weaver is working below the full price.' (3)

The evidence suggests that the strike had the overwhelming support of the Kilsyth weavers. When the strike was called they immediately set up a twenty-one strong committee to supervise its conduct. One of their first decisions was to advertise throughout the community their opposition to any lawbreaking. Not only were they strongly opposed to intimidation but went so far as to offer a reward to anyone who reported unlawful behaviour. This probably accounts for the fact that the 'excesses' were few and greatly exaggerated.

The question that comes to mind is why were men, already suffering great hardship, driven to strike for three months which was certain to drive them into destitution and debt as they were even denied access to the meagre Poor Law funds?

The strike was not a rash reaction. For some time weavers in Scotland, England and Ireland had been joining forces to protect their interests. Scotland generally, and Glasgow, the largest weaving centre in particular, took the lead in union organisation. This was not surprising since Scotland had a higher proportion of skilled weavers who were better educated and more articulate than was the case elsewhere in the United Kingdom. Weekly delegate meetings from all the main weaving centres in the United Kingdom had been taking place in Glasgow.

They had three simple objectives to bring stability to their trade and lives. Firstly, they were seeking a seven year apprenticeship and regulation on the transfer of journeymen to master weaver status. Secondly, they wanted to put an end to all fraud and embezzlement in the trade. Thirdly, they called upon magistrates to fix reasonable rates of wages for working in the cotton trade. It was this third objective that was to spark off the 1812 strike.

Although Kilsyth was in Stirlingshire the weavers trading links were with Glasgow, and they were very much part of the Glasgow campaign. It was that city that was to take the lead.

But to understand what was going on in Kilsyth it is worth taking a brief look at events prior to the strike. The Scottish weavers' union got a meeting in the Glasgow City chambers with the top manufacturers in the presence of the Lord Provost and magistrates. The weavers hoped the local authority would regulate the prices of cotton weaving in Glasgow but found the Council was as opposed to rate setting as the central government.

Then acting on the advice of the Whig advocate Francis Jeffrey the websters raised an action, based on old Scottish statutes, against a number of manufacturers before the Justices of the Peace in Glasgow. After examining an 'immense' number of witnesses the Justices considered the wage rates desired by the weavers to be 'moderate and reasonable.' (4)

The weavers then won another major legal triumph. After a long and costly action in the Court of Session, the Supreme Court in

Scotland affirmed the competence of Justices of the Peace to fix wage rates; but the sting was in the tail in that their judgment contained no clause compelling them to do so. The manufacturers ignored the judgment and continued to pay inferior wages.

Having won the moral, economic and legal battles the weavers were faced with the stark choice of abject surrender or strike action. They were careful in that even their decision to strike was kept within legal boundaries. There was case law which stated that workers who had applied to the Justices of the Peace and got their prices sanctioned had a right to strike in any numbers. It should be said that it was not only reverence for the law which moved the weavers to move with caution. They were well aware the establishment had no rational or legal cause to move against them, but any disorder would hand them the chance to discredit their cause.

In fact there was remarkably little unlawful conduct. Virtually no Luddite wrecking of machinery or property took place, as was the case in a number of English disputes. Impartial observers were impressed with the peaceful conduct of the weavers. One claimed that some weavers' complaints of intimidation arose out of a reluctance to anger their masters by admitting they had stopped work voluntarily. It was convenient to claim they were forced into strike action.

The trouble in Kilsyth came towards the end of the strike, and it began in the loom shop of John Young at Townhead. The outcome was that two leading officials of the Weavers Society, Matthew Stevenson and John McDougal were arrested and marched off to the Tolbooth in Stirling. Given the paranoia of the establishment at the time and the seriousness of the charges their prospects were alarming. There are no substantial differences in the accounts of what happened. But let us take John Young's testimony given in a precognition to the court, as he had the least cause to put the accused in a good light.

It reads:

'John Young weaver in New Town of Kilsyth being examined declares that he has been a weaver in Kilsyth for about 20 years, and is a member of the Weavers Society there.

That about three months ago the weavers in and about Kilsyth struck working because the manufacturers who employed them refused to pay them at the rates which had been proven to be fair and reasonable and approved by a sentence of the Justices of the Peace for Lanarkshire. That as their employers declined to pay these rates several of the weavers about Kilsyth, and the declarant amongst the rest, at last took work for such prices as they could get, because from their circumstances, and his having a numerous family, he could not afford to remain longer idle. That having got a web the declarant applied for and got one of the ravels belonging to the said society to beam his web.

That when we was preparing to do so on Thursday, January 21st last in the forenoon John McDougal, Alexander Miller, Matthew Stevenson and John Gilchrist, all weavers in Kilsyth, and Stevenson being also Postmaster and Gilchrist a Constable, all came into the declarant's workshop, when McDougal gave the declarant abusive language, and demanded the ravel which the declarant refused to give him, saying it was his own as long as he had occasion for it. That McDougal then laid hold of the ravel endeavouring to wrest it from the declarant which he resisted, and in the struggle it was broke. That McDougal damned the declarant for taking in the web below the table prices, and Stevenson also damned the declarant for a rotten hearted bugger and he would knock the declarant's head in the traddle holes if the ravel was his and take it from him by force.

That after the ravel was broke as aforesaid, McDougal again laid hold of the part of it in which the web was and said he would take it from him by force although he should destroy the web, when Gilchrist interfered and desired him not to hurt the web, upon which McDougal desisted and they all four went away, McDougal, or some of the rest, taking part of the ravel which was broke along with them.

That Thomas Shearer, weaver in Kilsyth, and Alexander Young, the declarant's son, a young man of 17 years of age, were in the declarant's shop on this occasion.

That after leaving the declarant's shop the above four persons went to the shop of John Graham, weaver and said Thomas Shearer and took away a ravel from each of their shops in their absence as these persons informed the declarant, and the said four persons afterwards and upon the same day went to the shop of William Wilson demanding a ravel from him but as his web was in it he refused to give it and went away without it and without using any violence, and of this the declarant was informed by Wilson.

That some day before the said persons came to the declarant's shop, as aforesaid, the said John McDougal had gone to the shop of Gabriel Anderson weaver in Kilsyth and after giving him some abusive language demanded his ravel which he took although there was a web in it at the time, but all this the declarant was only informed of by Anderson. That when McDougal demanded the declarant's ravel as aforesaid he said it was his, and this because a few days previous he was appointed by a meeting of the society to take charge of the ravels. That this meeting was called upon short notice when few members attended and McDougal was appointed although the time for which his predecessor was elected was not expired, and the declarant has heard for certain that McDougal refused to give ravels to some members of the society and gave them to others. That the declarant did not see any acts of violence committed by any of the operative weavers but has heard that the two webs in the shop of James Anderson were destroyed by vitriol in the course of the night but it is not known who did it. (It was of Friday last by squirting vitriol upon it through a broken pane of glass) and he also heard that some panes of glass in one or two shops were broken during the night there. (5)

The judgment appeared to precede the evidence. This precognition before the Sheriff Substitute of Stirlingshire was headlined 'Outrages committed by the operative weavers in Kilsyth'. On these flimsy accusations they planned to bring the full legal wrath of the establishment on the heads of Matthew Stevenson and John McDougal.

They were charged with 'combining and engaging not only not to work themselves, except at certain rates and prices, but with compelling others to join them by intimidation and threats of violence to their persons and property and also charging them with particular acts of violence.' It is clear even from the prosecution's main witness the issue was not coercion to stop colleagues working but action to prevent them from undermining their strike by the unauthorised use of the society's own machinery to do so. The reality was that the society's officials had every legal right to withdraw the reeds and ravels. The declared policy guidelines laid down by the weavers national leadership was that 'acting within the law beamers were imposed upon not to prepare webs for non strikers, and, on some occasions, ravels and other implements necessary for beaming webs be taken away from blacklegs.' (5)

The sum total of the dispute was that in a momentary outburst of anger between two men a ravel, which belonged to the society, was accidentally broken. As to the other hearsay accounts such as 'plots for breaking windows and destroying webs during the night' there was not a shred of evidence to link the accused.

Differences between the accused, however, emerged in the process. Matthew Stevenson, in evidence, explained their main purpose on the day of the incident was to borrow money for the Society. After McDougal had taken the ravels from Young and others he and John Gilchrist went to the house in Kingston, in Kilsyth, of James Baird, presumably another official of the society. Stevenson proposed that it was improper for McDougal 'in keeping the ravels' and that everybody should be allowed to work as they pleased. Before proceeding further he proposed they write a letter to McDougal for that purpose. The letter was duly written and taken to McDougal by Baird's apprentice.

We do not know McDougal's response but it is reasonable to assume that he saw this as a panic measure by Stevenson over the looming danger they were in which left McDougal more isolated.

The Kilsyth arrests were not regarded as an insignificant local matter. The Government scented blood. At least nine lengthy witness precognitions were secured by the Sheriff, and the all powerful Lord Advocate himself was directing the operation. Indeed, he thought it sufficiently important to write to Lord Sidmouth at the Home Office to brief him on developments. (6)

What saved the Kilsyth prisoners was not the obvious paucity of evidence but the timely negotiation of an amnesty to bring the strike to an end. However, Robert Anderson was probably correct in claiming the affair left lasting enmities that were taken to the grave.

It must have been a bitter experience for the weavers to return to work at the old exploitative pay, with debts accrued which they had no means to settle. But even the most pessimistic forecaster amongst them could not have foreseen the decades of struggle that lay ahead – draconian laws, armed insurrection, martyrdom and the slow decline and extinction of handloom weaving. A keynote battle had been lost but the war for democratic rights was entering a new, long and difficult phase.

The terms of the amnesty that brought the strike to an end are not known but at the conclusion of the twelve week strike fourteen strike leaders were indicted to stand trial; seven were sentenced to various period of imprisonment and four absconded, despite the fact that eminent Scottish lawyers were of the opinion that the weavers had broken no law.

The 1812 strike was not the first in the new industrial era. That took place 25 years earlier when the weavers of Calton, then a village to the east of Glasgow, demonstrated against a savage cut in payment rates. Six weavers were shot dead by the military. Their leader, James Granger, who was 38 years-old and with a family of six children, was tried in Edinburgh for 'forming an illegal combination'. He was sentenced to be publicly whipped through the streets of the city at the hands of the Common Executioner and was then to banish himself from Scotland for seven years. However, the resilient weaver was to return to Scotland and play an active part in the 1812 strike.

(1) Burns

(2) Anderson

(3) Murray, Norman *The Scottish Hand Loom Weavers: A Social History*

(4) Ibid p187

(5) Scottish National Archives Ref. A014/13/31

(6) Murray, Norman *The Scottish Hand Loom Weavers: A Social History*

CHAPTER 10

CAUTION SHOULD be exercised to avoid visiting our values and perspectives, particularly on those whose lives and experience are very different from our own. We all live situated lives. The matters that move and preoccupy us are not those that others would necessarily imagine. Even our sympathies can be misconstrued. As one great historian put it 'every age has its own consolations'. Just as today people can get more animated over the outcome of a football match than the prospect of the global financial order teetering on the brink of collapse, so also would our forefathers determine their own unique concerns.

For example the inter-church rivalry bubbled away, and despite the gathering economic gloom in 1816 there was another clash. Both the Relief and the established churches were strict Sabbatarians, but Fast Days, which were determined by the established church and enforced by the civic authorities, were a different matter. Robert Anderson recalls the observance of Fast Days meant a greater repression of human nature than the Sabbath did; 'even better keepit' was the phrase.

He claimed there is no exaggeration in the story of two shepherds who met at the boundary dyke of their respective parishes, and the one said to the other, 'Whustle on ma dowg, Bob, it's oor Fast Day'. The smile was more banished from the face than on Sabbath, the gait and demeanour were more expressive of grief, and no tongue made the most distant allusion to the things of this world. The church sermons were protracted, and the sermons were full of sin and misery. John Anderson instructed his congregation that Fast Days had not, like the Sabbath, a Divine origin and authority. It was purely a human institution, and that was enough for the weavers.

At the first sacrament after the opening of the new Parish Church in Backbrae the Kirk Session gave public notice that on the coming parish Fast Day no work was to be done, and that if any were found working they would be punished for contumacy.

'This was bringing in Caesar with a vengeance,' and the Relief weavers stiffened their backs and stood up to him. On the Fast morning constables were brought into the town and paraded the streets to see if anyone would be bold enough to drive a shuttle. They found them at it everywhere. Looms went 'clickity clack,' and shuttles flew with more than ordinary noise and speed. It was brave. There were the constables, the servants of the civil power, brought into the town to enforce submission to the State Church.

There was nothing worse to be feared than the jail. There was no danger of a stake being put up at the foot of the Meeting House Close to burn a weaver or two, but the jail was no joke for a man with a wife and family. However, there were no martyrs after all. Not a single weaver was handcuffed and taken over to Stirling. A newspaper of the day reported that 'when the constables went up Shuttle Street, they found that the weavers' looms were going at twice the ordinary rate.'

It may have been observed in this narrative that few local Radical leaders are identified by name, and for good reason. It is difficult for us to grasp in our age how great were the powers of the ruling land-owners and employers to take reprisals against those who offended them. Not least of those powers was exclusion from Poor Law Relief, the last line of survival when families were struck by disaster. The heritors, or landlords, were obliged by law to fund Poor Relief, and it was the duty of the Kirk Session to administer it.

But the Kilsyth Heritors were not prepared to surrender this power to others. They formed themselves into a sub-committee of the Kirk Session and kept rigid control of all expenditure. Reading the minutes of their meetings today they come across as cold as a fishmonger's slab, with the only priority being to minimise the cost to the heritors.

In one entry for 1817 it was reported that a baby had been abandoned by an 'unnatural' mother at Gateside. The meeting urged the Kirk Session to continue to make every effort to discover the mother, and it was clear that their efforts were not moved by concern for the health of the distressed mother. Meantime, the Session was instructed to take care of the child 'at as cheap a rate as possible'. At their next meeting in November it was reported that the baby had died. The Heritors graciously approved the cost of the baby's maintenance and burial in a pauper's grave. The meeting then went on to 'purge the casual list of the Poor they found expedient to strike-off.' (1)

The heritors such as the Edmonstones and Duke of Montrose, of course, did not attend these meetings personally, but at every meeting they had their lawyers and factors present to ensure their interests were served. The landlords, however, did have one brave critic, and a most surprising one at that, the Parish Minister, the Rev. Robert Rennie.

Parish ministers, who were appointed by the heritors, were normally submissive to their patrons, but Peter Anton informs us that Robert Rennie, who was minister at Kilsyth from 1789 until his death in 1820, 'spoke bitterly of the indifference' of the heritors regarding the upkeep of the poor. Indifference was not the correct term because the Kilsyth Heritors were anything but indifferent when it came to spending money, or more accurately not spending money. What Rennie was railing against was the miserly failure of the Heritors to fulfil their legal and moral duty to the poor.

Robert Rennie was the most unlikely rebel, being a reserved, good-natured and scholarly man besides being widely acknowledged as a distinguished scientist for his pioneering work in the conversion of peat moss into fuel and for agricultural purposes. Indeed, the legendary Russian Czar, Alexander 1st was so impressed by his work that he offered him the exalted post of Professor of Agriculture at the University of St. Petersburg, which he declined. But significantly he was also a born and bred Kilsythian who often boasted of his many relations in the Parish, which no doubt fuelled his indignation at the treatment of the poor.

He did, however, record one victory against the Heritors. By the 1800s the old Parish church at the cemetery, which had served Kilsyth for 256 years, was no longer fit for purpose. Matters came to a head before worship one Sabbath when two parishioners fought for possession of a pew. Dr. Rennie called a meeting to discuss the building of a new church, but knowing that this would entail spending money rather than saving it, not one of the Heritors attended. Undeterred, Robert Rennie took his case to the Presbytery. The outcome was the new Parish Church at Backbrae which was opened in 1816.

As noted earlier, the disputes between the churches had little to do with doctrine and everything to do with social and political values. Some years after the Fast Day burst-up we come across another crossing of swords. The then parish minister, the Rev. William Burns was on a visit to the family of Mr. John Goodwin at Barlandfauld House. The conversation turned to the condition of the handloom weavers, and the Reverend gentleman gravely observed that sixpence a day was a fair remuneration for the labours of a weaver, as being sufficient to furnish him with all the necessities of life. This moved local weaver and writer John Kirkwood to reply with this stinging epigram:

> The Church is in danger, the clergyman cries,
> The Church is in danger, each bigot replies.
> Should this appear strange, will it not appear stranger,
> If none will proclaim that the People's in danger,
> As placed in the hands of those minions of power,
> Who, under the long robe, Religion, devour,
> And who, when oppression embitters our state,
> *Insult* o'er the sufferings themselves did create.

But being a country community distant from the centre of manufacturing the Kilsyth weavers had another cause of distress which endured through the life of the industry – ruthless exploitation by the middle men. The weavers were dependant for work on local capitalists or agents. The 'Small Corks', as they were known, sold the finished cloth to various outlets and the agents were paid through commission by big Glasgow manufacturers. Both gave out webs, collected the finished cloth and paid the weavers, and both unscrupulously used the pool of labour as a weapon in their bitter competition with one another, cutting prices by cutting wage costs. Given the disparate nature and spread of the industry effective trade union defence against this exploitation eluded the weavers. As one weaver put it in evidence to a Parliamentary inquiry 'other trades being concentrated, can defend themselves very well. . . we being scattered over the whole face of the country cannot communicate with each other and are easily routed by our masters.' (2) They did not even have a platform to express their grievance until the radical journalist, Peter Mackenzie, launched the *Reformers Gazette* in the late 1820s; but then they made full use of the opportunity.

John Kirkwood lambasted the Corks and Agents in verse and prose. He wrote this sarcastic epigram 'on a weaving agent's eating a pound of flesh after dinner'.

> Tis strange the agents live so well,
> Or take such very hearty slices,
> Since every weaver here can tell,
> Their only aim is breaking prices. (3)

John Kirkwood bravely opened the onslaught in a letter to the *Reformers Gazette* in which he questioned why not a syllable had been said about that 'disinterested' body, the weaving agents, 'a race than whom none is more destructive of the public weal, at least as far as their influence is concerned'. He charged them with extortion and oppression exercised with unrelenting severity, pointing out that they took twenty-five per cent of the weavers' earnings. Even if the weaver received the full payment for his work, he claimed, it would scarcely supply the simple demands of nature, not to mention house rent and clothing. He promised and delivered further revelations of how the agents 'cozen the poor operative of his property and grow fat upon the ruin of their fellow creatures.' (4)

The country weavers were not only ripped-off in payments for their work but the agents operated a trucking system, running change houses and grocer shops, and charging twenty-five per cent more than goods could be bought in Glasgow. Their stranglehold was complete in that they could insist on the client weaver purchasing goods at their outlets under the threat of withdrawing work from those who refused.

As John Kirkwood put it, 'the weaver who is attached to an agent cannot send to the cheapest market, for he, poor devil, seldom or never handles the current coin of his own country, excepting at Whitsunday and Martinmas when perhaps a little money may be advanced to lull the infuriated laird.' (5)

There was one escape route from the iron embrace of the Corks and Agents for those sufficiently fit to take it. As Robert Anderson explained, 'they got their webs direct from Glasgow, wove them in their own loom shops, when finished, bundled them up, and tramped with them on their backs the intervening thirteen miles, got their money, with a new supply of web, and walked back, well pleased with their day's outing.' They had to face all weathers.

He recalled that in 1826, 'they toiled sweating, through the 'falls' with their burdens, amid a heat that rivalled that of the tropics. That year was long afterwards spoken of as the 'Short Corn Year', and in the far-off Craigends park my father's poor crop was not cut, but hand pulled'.

In the Spring the following year they faced extreme weather of a different kind. Robert Anderson was only three years-old at the time but remembered that weekend. 'It was the March Sacrament, and the dry, powdery pellets came on, with a North-East wind. It snowed all day and night on Saturday and all day and night on Sabbath and on into Monday.' His father's assistant minister arrived on his white pony from St. Ninians with a colleague on Saturday but there was no work for them to do on Sunday.

'No one could come to the church, and the Sacrament had to be deferred. The manse on Sabbath morning was drifted up to the top of its under windows. The weavers on the road that Saturday night had to struggle for their lives. In earlier days their forefolks had often to do the same. To think of these men, with their webs on their back, bending head down to the eastern drift, and staggering along the highway through the snow, serves as a glimpse of how it fared with our forefathers.'

Overshadowing all concerns, however, was the continuing decline in weavers' employment and income which was to gather pace following the end of the Napoleonic War in 1815. To place it in some perspective, from 1800 to 1808 wages were cut in half. In 1816 the Kilsyth weaver could make £1 per week, but by 1820 he was earning 11 shillings a week, with the notorious Corn Laws placing the purchase of bread beyond economic reach.

There is the mistaken view that handloom weaving was killed off by the advance of technology in mills. In fact this did not happen until much later in the 1800s. The paradox was that after 1815 as earnings slumped the number of weavers entering the industry grew markedly. Contributory factors were the influx of the unemployed from rural areas to the manufacturing cities; the flight of Highlanders escaping the Highland Clearances; the migration of Irishmen escaping poverty and oppression at home and the return of soldiers from the war to find themselves treated as 'seditious rabble and industrial scrap'.

Meantime, the reform movement crushed by the strike of 1812 and preoccupations of the War began to stir. It was two English reformers, Major John Cartwright and the radical journalist William Cobbett who were to blow the embers into a blazing flame. Cartwright had been a champion of reform throughout his long life and in 1812 had set up the Hampden Clubs in London to focus the campaign for reform. With other English reformers he had kept in close contact with his Scottish colleagues and in 1815 he embarked on a speaking tour of Scotland which attracted widespread support for reform.

Cobbett's weekly publication *The Political Register* became a rallying point for reformers keeping a sustained attack on the Government. Nowhere was the new call to the democratic cause joined with such enthusiasm as in central Scotland. It was around this time that the following event, taken from the local notes of James Stevenson by Robert Anderson, occurred.

'The political clubs, which had for a long time been meeting in secret, not only in Kilsyth, but in all the neighbouring towns and villages, resolved to have a united political gathering in demonstration of their strength. It was agreed to have it in Kilsyth. The place fixed on was a field in the North Barwood,

known subsequently for many a year as 'The Radical Park'.
Bonnybridge came afterwards. On the day agreed, contingents
arrived from Denny and Cumbernauld, and a large procession
from the west, composed of Kirkintilloch, Campsie, and
Balfron men, entered the town by Parkfoot, with flags, pipes
and drums. The town welcomed them with wild enthusiasm,
and marched with them, three abreast, up the Main Street,
along the market, and up the Craigends, to the Barwood. They
swarmed the Court Hill fifteen thousand strong. Mr James
Tansh was unanimously voted to preside. He wore on his head
the French cap of liberty, a red velvet one, tasselled and
embroidered, made and presented by a Kilsyth lady Reformer,
whose name, surely, might have been preserved, but it is not.
My brother William, then a stripling, made his debut that day,
not in person, but by proxy. He wrote the speech, but Alexander
Abercrombie delivered it from the top of a big boulder stone.
The welkin rang with shouts, as speaker after speaker addressed
the throng in burning denunciation of the people's wrongs and
the authors of them. Over at Colzium House was the
(Edmonstone) factor, with some friends, standing on the lawn
and listening to the hurrahs that came on the breeze from the
crowd, and he is credited with having wished for a cannon to
scatter them. . .'

But as the people rallied to the Democratic cause they were not to
know that two merciless and unrelenting enemies of reform were about
to confront them – Lord Castlereagh, Foreign Secretary and Leader
of the House of Commons, the hammer of democrats at home and
abroad, and Lord Sidmouth, Home Secretary and architect of the
infamous spy system that was about to be unleashed.

Soon many become convinced that peaceful persuasion directed
at a Government that refused to listen would be of no avail. Support
grew for armed struggle and a new fearful chapter of militancy and
repression began.

This was probably the period that Robert Anderson was referring
to when he wrote,

'In Kilsyth the weavers made pikes, a favourite Scottish weapon of war ever since Bruce taught his soldiers to use it so well against the English invaders on the field of Bannockburn. The authorities came to know what was being done at the smiddy fires in the town. One morning early the Relief manse was startled by the Yeomanry searching for hidden weapons in the garden behind. Down in the village old swords were scoured up, and guns, cleaned of rust, had their flint locks oiled. It was all done 'hiddlins', for, truth to tell, there was fear in every heart as there was danger at every door. The swords, pikes and guns were only to be used in the last extremity. A weaver, who was polishing an old claymore, startled by the sudden opening of the loomshop door, quickly plunged the gleaming steel over the hilt into a barrel that stood near him, filled with flour paste, made up for 'dressing the web'. The country was over-run with Government spies. No Kilsyth man was ever suspected as belonging to the hated brotherhood, but all visitors to the town were dangerous whether clad in moleskin or broadcloth. . . Richmond the spy was the best hated name in those days in the west of Scotland. He was the reputed head of the dreaded fraternity. Everyone heard of him, everyone talked of him, nobody saw him. He was a minor sort of devil, impersonal as his chief, and similarly feared.'

The struggle for democracy was about to enter a new, dark and eventful phase.

---

(1) Kilsyth Heritors minutes (1813-1814)
(2) Parliamentary papers 1834 Vol. X p73
(3) *Weavers Journal* 1st December 1836
(4) *Reformers Gazette* 23rd April 1832 (p351)
(5) *Reformers Gazette* May 1832 (p412)

RICHMOND THE SPY was one Alexander Richmond, and it was not that the weavers did not know him. They knew him only too well. He was a weaver from Pollokshaws and one of the organisers of the 1812 strike who had been outlawed at the end of the strike after fleeing to England to escape arrest. On his return he was given a minimum one month prison sentence. What the weavers fatally did not know for almost a year was that on this return Richmond had been recruited as a government spy by Kirkman Finlay, the Glasgow businessman and Tory MP. Even after he was unmasked as a spy he remained a deadly threat as he had set up a network of treacherous informers within the Reform movement. Kilsyth weavers in particular had good cause to fear Richmond.

There was a development at that time which was to confuse the Government then, and trouble historians now; the Reform movement had split into two broad camps – the old moral force camp who believed in campaigning within the law for change and a new force committed to armed struggle to resist oppression and seek reform. Richmond was in fact only one of a number of paid spies who was feeding the Government information but, as Government records reveal, it was Richmond who 'provided evidence of an entirely different association which he obtained from his friend on the Central Committee and different Masonic friends'.

He reported that:

> 'there were 50 different associations in the West of Scotland from Paisley to Kilsyth, Campsie and Airdrie. They acted in consort and their object was the 'complete overthrow' of existing arrangements and seizure of the property of the higher classes of society.

'To obtain their objects they had 60 to 100 stores of arms and
supplies of powder and ball, as well as a number of cutlasses.
The plan was to seize the barracks and thus obtain more arms
and ammunition, partly overpowering and partly bringing over
the soldiers.' (1)

The accuracy of reports by Richmond and other spies have to be
treated with caution. They had a vested interest in exaggeration and
falsehood as their payments were influenced by how valuable the
Government assessed their information. For example, there is not a
jot of evidence to support the claim that the reformers had changed
their democratic demands to include 'the complete overthrow of
existing arrangements and the seizure of property.' He was correct,
however, in identifying and revealing the formation of a network of
new militant Union Societies (not to be confused with trade union
bodies) who were prepared to break loose from the shackles of the
law. He alarmed the Government further by revealing that the new
societies were operating in close contact with English radicals, and
he provided the secret oath taken by recruits to the new societies. It
was modelled on the oath of the United Scotsmen, which itself was
adopted from the United Irishmen.

'In the awful presence of God, I do solemnly swear that I will
persevere in my endeavouring to form a Brotherhood of
affection amongst Britons of very description, who are
considered worthy of confidence; and I will persevere in my
endeavours to obtain for all the people in Great Briton and
Ireland not disqualified by crimes or insanity, the elective
franchise at the age of 21, with free and equal representation
and annual parliaments; and that I will support the same to
the utmost of my power, either by moral or physical strength,
or force, as the case may require. And I do solemnly swear that
neither hopes, fears, rewards or punishments shall induce me
to inform on, or give evidence against any member or
members collectively or individually, for any act or expression
done or made, in or out, in this or similar societies, under the

punishment of death to be inflicted on me by any member or members of such societies. So help me God, and keep me steadfast.' (2)

The build-up to the 1820 insurrection had begun. Richmond and his acolytes who infiltrated the democratic movement posing as radicals began to gather evidence and identify democrats for arrest.

It is evidence of the enduring relevancy of those distant conflicts that modern perceptions influence their interpretation today. The authors of the *The Scottish Insurrection of 1820* (3) stand accused by other historians of the period, such as Dr. W.M. Roach of grossly overstating the Scottish independence motivation of those early democrats, although concerns over Scottish identity and culture were a sub-text in those and other struggles. One historian bluntly accuses them of confusing nationalism with patriotism; if true it would not have been the first or the last time. Also disputed is their central claim that the Scottish Insurrection was planned in its entirety by the Government to lure the democrats into open rebellion, as official papers of the time indicated the Government was as surprised by the unfolding events as everyone else. On the other hand, Dr. Roach's claim that Richmond was employed as a spy and not as an *agent provocateur*, while being true, it does not follow that he did not act as an *agent provocateur*; indeed there is compelling evidence that he did.

As the campaign for democracy entered its most dramatic and tragic phase the reformers had a rare but significant victory. On a summer's night in July 1817 Glasgow weaver Andrew McKinlay was trudging along the track road from Edinburgh to Glasgow. He was returning to his wife and eight children and a life of hardship, poverty and hunger, yet he was the happiest man in the Kingdom. The night mail coach went rattling past carrying before him the news of his remarkable escape from the gallows. McKinlay was a leader of the Calton Weavers Society, and had spent five months imprisoned in Edinburgh Castle along with his friend and colleague John Campbell, both charged with High Treason. Twenty other democrats were also in prison awaiting trial but McKinlay's was set up as the show trial.

McKinlay and Campbell were kept apart and defence lawyers were denied access to Campbell. Then it was made known that Campbell was to give evidence for the prosecution against his friend. Was ever a man so wretched as Andrew McKinlay? He had been personally entrapped by Richmond into signing the 'treacherous oath' and now the noose was being put around his neck by the betrayal of his friend and colleague. But then John Campbell succeeded in smuggling a note through to McKinlay enclosed in a quid of tobacco. It stated: 'They are wanting to bribe me to swear away your life, but I'm true.'

At the opening of the trial (4) McKinlay's lawyer, the Whig advocate and reformer Francis Jeffrey, who had given his services free, accused the Crown of bribing a witness. When Campbell entered the witness box the presiding judge asked him:

'Have you any malice or ill will to the prisoner at the bar?'

'None, my Lord,' replied Campbell.

'Has anyone given you any reward or promise of reward for being a witness in this trial?'

Campbell stunned the court by replying, 'Yes, my Lord.'

Taken aback, Lord Hermond repeated the question and warned Campbell to think carefully about his answer. Campbell replied that Deputy Lord Advocate Drummond, in the presence of the Sheriff of Edinburgh, had tried to bribe him to give incriminating evidence against McKinlay. He was to get a good permanent Government situation abroad through Lord Sidmouth after he had given evidence that day for the prosecution. It was a brave and masterful stroke that immediately turned the accusers into the accused.

With the world looking on the Crown had to abandon their case, and the charges against all the other prisoners were dropped. Henry Cockburn, a friend and colleague of Francis Jeffrey, who was later to become a judge of the Court of Session, said: 'The result of that trial protected for a time the liberties of Scotland.'

The release of McKinlay and the other prisoners, who belonged to the same wing of the movement as the Kilsyth weavers, would have been celebrated in Kilsyth and, indeed, throughout the movement.

Seventeen years later when the *Reformers Gazette* exposed more details of the spy network Richmond wrote to the magazine from his home in London in an attempt to whitewash his reputation. He boasted of his 'practical benevolence towards mankind'. In the following edition Andrew McKinlay replied stating that he was an instance of his practical benevolence:

'for it was through his hellish contrivances that I was entrapped. He hatched the Treasonable Oath that pleased Sidmouth and Castlereagh so much, and then he found me lodgings for it in Glasgow Jail – from that he got me quarters in Edinburgh Castle, and relying on his award, he no doubt expected to see my body upon a gibbet, and my head upon a spike; and this is the specimen of his practical benevolence towards me and my wife and eight children. My heart swells when I reflect on the dreadful pangs I have undergone in that business.'

He concluded by congratulating the editor on 'exposing the villain in all his deformity.'

The editor added a postscript to the letter saying, 'something should be done for this unfortunate man. We learn that he is now in a most miserable condition – literally starving'. (5) McKinlay's letter reveals that the weavers believed, rightly or wrongly, that Richmond not only used the secret oath to entrap democrats but was the author of the document.

The arrival of the new Union Societies lifted the battle onto a new and dangerous level. It was recognition of the stark choice posed to the democrats, either abject surrender or armed struggle against the imperial might of a corrupt tyranny. Even those who had firmly eschewed all action outside the law had to acknowledge this reality.

The escalation from exhortation to physical force gained growing support. Around the same time as Andrew McKinlay was fighting for his life an assassination attempt was made on the Prince Regent, the Prince of Wales, when on his way to open Parliament. He had assumed the Regency in 1811 when his father George III became irredeemably mad and in 1820 became King George IV on the death of his father. He was despised across the political spectrum for his extravagant, dissolute and self-indulgent lifestyle. He gambled without restraint, kept numerous mistresses, fathered a number of illegitimate children and at one point built up personal debts which equalled in today's valuation a staggering £49 million, which the taxpayer had to pay. All this was going on against the background of the people, who he held in contempt, struggling against unemployment and hunger. On his death in 1830 *The Times* did not water down its verdict. It stated in an editorial: 'There never was an individual less regretted by his fellow creatures than this diseased king. What eye has wept for him? What heart has heaved one throb of unmercenary sorrow? If he ever had a friend we protest that the name of him or her has never reached us.'

Nevertheless, the assassination attempt sent a tremor of apprehension through the establishment. If the head of state could be targeted by the more militant elements of the rebels who could feel safe?

However, it would be an error to assume that either Thomas Muir's Friends of the People or the later democrats of the 1800s were republicans in the modern sense. It was the Tory Government and the electoral system they opposed, not the institution of Royalty.

But for most the defining event of the age was the Peterloo Massacre. On a hot, cloudless August summer day in 1819 between 60,000 and 80,000 people gathered in St. Peter's Field, Manchester to hold a peaceful demonstration for political reform. The event promoted by the Manchester Patriotic Union was well organised. The declared aim was that the gathering should be as 'morally effective as possible'. Demonstrators were urged to wear their best clothes and weapons of offence or defence were strictly forbidden. 'Cleanliness, sobriety, order and peace were to be exercised'.

As the rally got underway the magistrates, who were looking on from a nearby house, ordered the arrest of the platform party. The Manchester and Salford Yeomanry, who were described as the 'younger members of the Tory Party in arms' were stationed close by in Portland Street. When they received the order they immediately drew their swords and galloped towards St. Peter's Field. One trooper, in a frantic effort to catch up knocked down a woman in the street causing her child to be thrown from her arms to his death. Two year old William Fildes was the first casualty of Peterloo.

The crowd around the speakers was so dense that 'their hats

seemed to touch.' As the inexperienced horses were thrust further and further into the crowd towards the platform they reared and plunged as people desperately tried to get out of their way. The soldiers who were now out of control 'were cutting everyone they could reach'. When the blood-soaked field was cleared 15 people were dead and over 600 wounded, 168 of them being women.

The unprovoked slaughter shocked the nation. The reformers were further enraged by the response to the Peterloo Massacre, named in ironic comparison to the Battle of Waterloo fought four years earlier. A test case was brought against four members of the Manchester Yeomanry but all were acquitted as the court ruled their action had been justified to disperse an illegal gathering. Far from condemning the mass murder the Government prosecuted and imprisoned the organisers and speakers at the rally. Lord Sidmouth conveyed to the magistrates the thanks of the Prince Regent for their action in the 'preservation of the public peace'.

The poet Shelley who got the news of the massacre in Italy composed a chilling but resounding commemoration of the event, the *Masque of Anarchy*.

> As I lay asleep in Italy
> There came a voice from over the Sea,
> And with great power it forth led me
> To walk in the visions of Poesy.
>
> I met Murder on the way –
> He had a mask like Castlereagh –
> Very smooth he looked, yet grim;
> Seven blood-hounds followed him:
>
> All were fat; and well they might
> Be in admirable plight,
> For one by one, and two by two,
> He tossed the human hearts to chew
> Which from his wide cloak he drew.

Clothed with the Bible, as with light,
And the shadows of the night,
Like Sidmouth, next, Hypocrisy
On a crocodile rode by.

And many more Destructions played
In this ghastly masquerade,
All disguised, even to the eyes,
Like Bishops, lawyers, peers, or spies.

Shelley concluded the 91 verse commemoration, which many regard as the greatest political poem written in English, with a call to action:

Rise like Lions after slumber
In unvanquishable number –
Shake your chains to earth like dew
Which in sleep had fallen on you –
Ye are many – they are few.

In Scotland large-scale demonstrations and rallies were reported in the main radical centres, Ayr, Kilsyth, Paisley, Claynowes, Glasgow and Neilston where collections were made to help the Peterloo victims. At Airdrie a whole band was arrested for playing *Scots Wha Hae*.

'The utmost tranquillity characterised all of the meetings. The processions were splendid and every precaution it appears has been taken to prevent irritation and alarm, even in the minds of the most alarmable,' reported a new radical weekly paper, *The Spirit of the Union* (a reference to the Radical Union Societies) which was set up to give the democrats a public platform. However, it lasted only eleven issues before it was suppressed by the Government, and its editor, Gilbert MacLeod, was sentenced to five years transportation to Botany Bay. He was to die long before his sentence expired. (6) One rally which was reported extensively gives a flavour of the events. At the start a band played *God Save the King*, followed *by Rule Britannia* and *Scots Wha Hae*, then a speaker recited the following lines:

> May the Rose of England never bloom
> May the Thistle of Scotland never grow
> May the Harp of Erin never play
> Till Hunt, the champion gains the day.

Hunt was Henry Hunt, the main speaker at Peterloo who was in prison awaiting trial. There was a pole bearing a cap of liberty, and poles bearing a bundle of rods tied with crape, emblematic of unity in reform.

With the country in a state of ferment a wise and responsible government would have been expected to take action to lower the temperature; this government did the opposite. On November 23rd 1819 Sidmouth and Castlereagh pushed through what was known as the Six Acts, against strong opposition from the Whigs. They were designed to crush the democrats. The draconian measures included banning meetings and assemblies, imposing a tax on radical publications, heavy prison sentences and transportation for 'blasphemous and seditious libels' and changes in the administration of justice system to accelerate prosecutions. But even before the notorious legislation was passed the democrats were planning armed resistance. The count-down to the Insurrection of 1820 had begun.

(1) Roach, W.M. 'Alexander Richmond and the Radical Reform Movements in Glasgow in 1816-17' *Scottish Historical Review* Vol. 51 No.151 Part 1 (April 1972) pp11-19
(2) Berresford, P. and Mac A'Ghobhainn, Seumas *The Scottish Insurrection of 1820*
(3) Ibid
(4) Stewart, William *Selection From the Writings* Published by Robert Gibson & Sons (Glasgow) Ltd. 1948
(5) *Reformers Gazette* May 3rd 1835
(6) Berresford, P. and Mac A'Ghobhainn, Seumas *The Scottish Insurrection of 1820*

CHAPTER 12

ON A COLD winter Monday morning in December 1819 three hundred fully armed men marched into Kilsyth to join up with local weavers. Not before, or since, has a group of men met in Kilsyth imbued with such serious purpose. Their plan, no less, was to march on Glasgow to join an insurrection with the aim of not only sweeping away the British Government but changing the whole political order for ever.

That morning in Glasgow 'a vast number of idle people, and mostly strangers among them, perambulated the streets'. The early part of the morning showed the roads leading into Glasgow to be crowded with people heading in the direction of the city. The city was also bristling with soldiers and heavy weapons because the planned date of the insurrection, December 13th, was probably the worst kept secret in the annals of conflict. But despite the resolute courage and the long and painstaking preparation by the democrats the enterprise was to end in anti-climax.

As the Kilsyth army prepared to march off to Glasgow a dispatch arrived from the city stating the insurrection had been suspended. They had no option but to disband and return home, with all the dangers that entailed. The Government had been well prepared for conflict. The previous day the military commander-in-chief Sir Thomas Bradford had travelled with his staff from Edinburgh to Glasgow. It is an indication of how thoroughly the ranks of the democrats had been penetrated that Lord Hope, Lord President of the Court of Session, appears to have known of the suspension of the insurrection the day before the Kilsyth weavers. He informed Lord Melville:

'the letters from Glasgow this morning say that the report is that the insurrection will not take place tomorrow. This is all good, if it is not to take place. But it is very vexatious if it is to take place at last – for the troops will be harassed to death on the one hand, while every attempt will be made to reduce them on the other.'

He went on to express concern that while the troops were absent from Edinburgh 'an attempt will be made to incite a Rising here'. The day after the planned insurrection Lord Hope wrote again to Melville. He put the cancellation of the Rising down to 'the imposing appearance of the troops, on which the Radicals had not at all calculated, which disconcerted and overawed them and the Rising was countermanded'. (1)

But that was not the reason. What Lord Hope did not appear to know was that delegates from four counties had convened in Glasgow to direct the rising. They were waiting for news from England that a rebellion had been launched there, but when no news came they decided to postpone. (2)

Lord Hope had been fully briefed on events in Kilsyth. He went on to comment: 'that 300 men had marched into Kilsyth fully armed, en route for Glasgow, but hearing all was quiet there had disbanded'. He disclosed that he had written to the Solicitor General in Glasgow to 'urge strongly the propriety of making a thorough search for arms, before the troops were drawn off – and to call on the people by a strong proclamation to bring in and surrender their arms, as was done in Ireland, and to warn that if arms were found concealed by them after such notice, they would be prosecuted with the utmost vigour of the law'.

Great hopes had been invested in the Rising, and with its suspension the Government expected sporadic outbursts of frustrated violence. In fact the West of Scotland was remarkably quiet except in Kilsyth where special factors prevailed. On Sunday, the eve of the planned insurrection, three Kilsyth men were arrested, one for making pikes and two for placing orders for pikes. The three were seized and taken to Stirling Jail and warrants were issued for the arrest of thirty others.

As news of the arrests spread and the suspension of the Rising on Monday the town exploded in anger. The Government-backing *Glasgow Chronicle* reported that despite two troops of soldiers being berthed at the Durntreath Arms Hotel and the presence of the local Yeomanry, 'the radicals went parading the streets in hundreds. They were from all quarters throwing stones and snowballs at the yeomen'. Even the parish minister, Dr. Rennie, was caught up in the fray 'as they threw snowballs at him in such a manner he would have fallen to the ground had he not been assisted. Also the radicals fired six shots opposite the Inn; one ball was within three inches of entering the window where an officer was.'

The *Glasgow Chronicle's* breathless correspondent went on: 'You have no idea of the state of Kilsyth. We have no less than four troops of horsemen this night.' (Tuesday 14th) (3)

But the arrests had all the signs of a deliberate provocation by the Government forces. Had the arrests been genuine, the investigation and administration of warrants would have taken at least several days. Why did they wait until the eve of the planned Rising, and on the Sabbath too, to make the arrests if it was not an attempt to wrong-foot the weavers by provoking them into precipitous revolt? Not, of course, that their suspicions about weapons were unfounded. In Kilsyth, as in many other communities, weapons were being made, acquired and stored for some time along with extensive military drilling and training. However, it must have been a nightmare scenario for the organisers of the uprising. The last thing they would have wanted was their carefully laid plans disrupted by a premature conflict outside the city. The following day there was no sign of protest which suggests that by then the leaders were back in control.

As the new search for weapons was launched, Kilsyth was an obvious target. Within days of the aborted Insurrection it was officially reported that:

> 'yesterday at half-past one o'clock the Sheriff Depute and other
> civil officers, assisted by a party of the 10th Hussars, the
> Kilsyth Yeomanry and a party of the veterans marched into
> Kilsyth and searched many houses for arms, when they found

one pike, a few shafts, and a quantity of gun bullets buried in a garden, and two muskets concealed in a dunghill.' (4)

But the democrats were also active. Only three days after the Rising was called off a new committee of seven was established, with delegates from Ayr, Kilmarnock, Mauchline, Paisley, Airdrie, Kilsyth and Campsie 'to supervise measures of reform'. Lord Hope was not far off the mark when he wrote to Melville on December 17th to say: 'the people are rife for rebellion as ever, and only in sullen and sultry silence waiting for a more convenient opportunity'.

The following month the old King George III died and the 58 year-old profligate and reactionary Prince Regent became George IV. Only a few weeks later another insurrection was attempted, this one at the centre of power in London. A quite separate extremist group laid plans to ignite a revolution by assassinating the entire Government whilst they were dining at Lord Harrowby's house in Grosvenor Square on February 23rd. The plot was to follow the assassinations by seizing the bank area of the city and taking canons which had been placed there. At the same time various buildings were to be set alight to create the maximum confusion and the Mansion House was to be taken over as the seat of a new Provisional Government.

But Government agents had infiltrated the organisation and on the day of the Rising twenty-five conspirators met in a house in Cato Street. Suddenly the house was surrounded by soldiers and after a struggle nine men were arrested. Five were tried and executed, including the leader, Arthur Thistlewood. Five others were transported for life.

---

(1) *The Scottish Insurrection 1820*
(2) Roach
(3) *Glasgow Chronicle* 16th December 1819
(4) H.O. Scotland 102-Volume 32 1820 Part III

CHAPTER 13

DRACONIAN LAWS were defied as angry protest gatherings took place in many parts of Scotland. By now no-one on either side was in any doubt that the armed struggle was suspended – not abandoned. The weavers in Kilsyth and in many places throughout the West of Scotland awoke on Sunday morning, 1st April 1820, to find a proclamation on the walls of prominent buildings calling for an immediate general strike as a prelude to a general Insurrection. The proclamation by order of the Committee of Organisation for forming a Provisional Government, addressed to the Inhabitants of Great Britain and Ireland, began:

> 'Friends and Countrymen: – Roused from that torpid state in which we have been sunk for so many years, we are, at length, compelled, from the extremity of our sufferings, and the contempt heaped upon our Petitions for redress, to assert our Rights, at the hazard of our lives and proclaim to the world the real motives, which (if not misrepresented by designing men, would have United all ranks) have reduced us to take up arms for the redress of our Common Grievances.
>
> The numerous Public Meetings held throughout the Country have demonstrated to you that the interests of all Classes are the same. That the protection of the Life and Property of the Rich Man is in the interest of the Poor Man, and in return, it is in the interest of the Rich to protect the Poor from the iron grip of despotism, for, when its victims are exhausted in the lower circles, there is no assurance that its ravages will not be continued in the upper. For once set in motion, it will continue to move till a succession of Victims fall.
>
> Our principles are few, and founded on the basis of our

Constitution which was purchased with the DEAREST BLOOD of our ancestors, and which we swear to transmit to posterity unsullied, or perish in the attempt. Equality of Rights (not Property) is the object for which we contend, and which we consider is the only security for our liberties and Lives.
Let us show to the world that we are not the lawless sanguinary Rabble which our Oppressors would persuade the higher circles we are – but a Brave and Generous People, determined to be Free. Liberty or Death is our motto, and We have sworn to return home in triumph – or return no more!'

It went on to appeal to soldiers to join the reformers and to take strike action until they 'are in possession of those Rights which distinguish Freemen from Slaves.' But it also warned those who would take up arms against their efforts to 'regenerate their country, and restore its inhabitants to their native dignity, that they would be regarded as traitors to their country, and enemies to their King.'

In Kilsyth the proclamation was posted on the doors of the Parish Church, the Relief Church and other prominent buildings causing great excitement as it was believed that at last the day of deliverance had arrived. As one historian stated. 'The address was displayed not only in prominent radical centres such as Glasgow, Paisley and Kilsyth, but throughout south west Scotland.' (1)

Immediately 60,000 people in and around Glasgow stopped working but many were to return to work within a short period as nothing appeared to happen and rumours spread that the Rising was a Government scheme of entrapment. This was not the case in Kilsyth, however, where weavers on reading the address 'laid down their shuttles and for several days paraded the streets.' (2) This information was passed on by Matthew Stevenson the Kilsyth Postmaster in another letter, written the day following the posting of the Proclamation. Matthew Stevenson briefed William Kerr, his Postmaster in Edinburgh.

He wrote:

Yesterday being the Sabbath, the most serious and atrocious

printed placard by way of address to the nation was posted on the walls of the Parish Kirk and Relief Meeting House, and on other houses of the town calling on the nation to rebel and threatening all those who carried arms against their country (as they were pleased to call it) with death, and ordering all public works to stop after the first of April; and this day the whole body of weavers here were idle and parading the streets. When they intend to resume work I cannot learn but our Yeoman Cavalry has been on duty this day, and I understand some of them have been armed and out ('out' was a Scottish term meaning in open rebellion).

We have in this place a great many ill-disposed men who, I believe, would commence plundering if they thought of succeeding, and from all I can learn they are waiting on intelligence from England about a blow to be struck there, and then they will begin generally here and in all the west country. I think from their appearance they have a very infuriated look and God only knows what will be the consequence. Yet, I hope the civil forces, supported by the military, will be able to overcome them. Our Special Constables, of whom I am one, I believe, must make their appearance, and I do believe that many have arms of defence of one kind or another. I learn that our Yeomanry is to patrol our streets through the night. If anything occurs I will not fail to let you know.

I am, Sir,

Your Honour's,

Most faithful and obedient servant,

Matthew Stevenson

His letter, of course, was passed on to Lord Sidmouth at the Home Office. We can only speculate about the role of Matthew Stevenson. It is unlikely that he was a spy, but he was an informer. The most likely explanation is that he was instructed by his employer to provide information, but it is worthy of note that he did not name names and the information he passed to the authorities they already had. However, one item of news he probably inadvertently supplied would have been of interest to the Government, if only to confirm what they had already been told. That was the reference to them 'waiting on intelligence from England'.

In the week following the Proclamation the tension was palpable all over west central Scotland and there were a number of minor clashes with the military. Adam Cochrane, a young Paisley weaver was shot dead, and when a crowd threw stones at soldiers as they attempted to remove the address from a wall in Paisley, they opened fire wounding several and killing a woman who was shot through the neck. Later in the week the military charged a crowd with fixed bayonets wounding several and killing an old man. One incident which was to have grave consequences later took place in Duke Street, Glasgow, when a Justice of the Peace attempted to pull down a copy of the address.

Andrew Hardie, a 26 year-old weaver who lived with his parents nearby in High Street and who was a member of the Castle Street Radical Union Society, stepped forward and told the justice to the cheers of the crowd, 'before I permit you to take down yon notice I will part with the last drop of my blood.' The Justice and his party were forced to retreat. Hardie's stand was brave but was to prove costly.

One of the enduring unresolved mysteries of the whole saga was the role and fate of the twenty-eight man Committee of Organising a Provisional Government who were already in military custody after being arrested on March 21st at a meting in the Gallowgate. They remained in custody until November, yet no trace of who they were and what became of them has been discovered despite rigorous research. This has fuelled the belief that the whole attempted Insurrection was planned by the Government to lure the democrats into the open. Was there a conspiracy, and if so how far up the ranks of the Government did it run? At what point does entrapment by spies become a conspiracy? These questions remain a subject of debate.

But during the stand-off that week events were unfolding. On Tuesday Duncan Turner informed the leaders of the Glasgow Societies of the plans for the Rising. It would begin on Wednesday morning, and the sign would be the failure of the mail coach from London to arrive in Glasgow. A messenger had been sent to Strathaven to raise the democrats there who were ordered to march to Cathkin Braes where 5,000 men would be gathered for an attack on the city. Another strong division was gathering at Campsie to launch an attack from the north. Turner wanted 200 men from Glasgow to march to Condorrat to join with local radicals and march on to the Carron Ironworks near Falkirk where the workforce were on strike. They would hand over two pieces of cannon and a large quantity of arms and ammunition. The Radicals were then to return through Kilsyth and join up with local Radicals and march on to Glasgow.

The plan was strikingly similar to the earlier aborted Rising with Kilsyth the last gathering point for the march on Glasgow. It certainly made strategic sense to travel via Condorrat then cut across country to Carron, thus by-passing Kilsyth where the Kilsyth Yeomanry were based, and where it would be anticipated that Regular soldiers would be sent to reinforce them, as indeed they were. If our reasoning is correct it would suggest that the overall plan to attack Carron was devised by the Democrats and infiltrated by Government spies, rather than the whole operation being devised by the Government as a plan of entrapment. There was clearly more dialogue, planning and talks going on amongst the weavers of central Scotland which, for security reasons, were not recorded. In this connection, the Airdrie Weavers Society appointed a delegate to Kilsyth 'and other towns to report on progress on the Bonnymuir campaign' which suggests that much of the activity was taking place here.

However plausible and thrilling the plan sounded, the only problem was that Turner, who purported to be a member of the Provisional Government, was in fact one of four spies recruited by the Government in the Glasgow area. Turner had several meetings with Glasgow Radical leaders that Tuesday, the last one taking place in Clyde Street around midnight. There was a debate as a growing number of men wisely withdrew on the grounds that it was not feasible for such a small number of ill-equipped men to attack Scotland's largest industrial complex, and they were not convinced by Turner's assurance that they would be joined by many others along the route. In the end only around thirty men agreed to take part and Turner personally asked Andrew Hardie to take command of the party. He gave him one half of a split card and told him a man at Condorrat would present him with the corresponding half of the card; that man was to take command of the operation at Carron. The small intrepid party then set out for Condorrat and Turner disappeared into the night never to be seen again.

Around 11pm on the same night the household where John Baird lived with his brother and sister-in-law in Condorrat were awakened by knocking at the door. Mrs. Baird found a man on the doorstep in driving rain who introduced himself as John Andrews, and he asked to see John Baird. Inside, he presented credentials as a messenger from the Provisional Government; he was later to be exposed as John King the leader of the group of four spies. As Mrs. Baird revived the dying fire to dry off his soaking clothes, and prepare food King outlined the plan and invited John Baird to take command, to which he agreed. He passed over the other half of the split card to identify the leader of the Glasgow group who would arrive before the break of dawn. Then as John Baird went out in the stormy night to alert the local Radicals, King slept in his bed. Around 5am the Glasgow party arrived in the village and King introduced Baird and Hardie.

The two men were said to have struck up an immediate rapport. However, only ten local men arrived. The combined force when they left Condorrat was only thirty-five poorly armed men. John Baird, who had been chosen to command the group based on his seven years military experience, including service at the Battle of Waterloo, had serious misgivings about attempting the operation with so few men, but King persuaded him to continue saying that he would go ahead and raise the Radicals at Camelon and Falkirk who would join them along with a group who were on their way from Anderston. The small army then set off from Condorrat in military order. They stopped a few miles along the way at the Castlecary Bridge Tavern where Baird ordered breakfast of two penny loaves and porter, a dark sweet ale. Suitably refreshed they marched on.

Baird then decided to split the party into two groups to ensure they did not miss the colleagues expected to join them; one group would proceed along the road while the other went along the bank of the Forth and Clyde Canal. Hardie took charge of the party going along the turnpike road, and he called at various houses to supplement their arms and ammunition. One householder at Longcroft objected to the seizure of two muskets and a quantity of ammunition but Hardie took them nevertheless and gave the man a receipt signed on behalf of the Provisional Government. As they left the village they met an English traveller on horseback who told them he was on his way to Glasgow. Hardie advised him to keep clear of Glasgow which was in a state of revolution, but they allowed him to go on his way.

But another man was on the road that morning, Private Nicol Hugh Baird, a civil engineer from Kelvinhead and a mounted trooper of the Kilsyth Yeomanry. He rode into Kilsyth and into the cobbled courtyard of the local inn where a troop of the 10th Hussars, commanded by Lt. Ellis Hodgson, were resting. Lt. Hodgson was talking to Lt. James Davidson, a Tory lawyer from Edinburgh who was in command of the Kilsyth Yeomanry, when the breathless Baird entered to relate his heroic adventure. He told how on the road he had come upon a large body of armed insurgents who had fired at him, and how, single-handed, he had attacked them and drove them off and then rode to Kilsyth with the news. He was to give evidence to this effect at the trial later, but in a letter smuggled out of prison Andrew Hardie exposed Baird as a liar and perjurer and his evidence as a farrago of self-aggrandised fabrications. He wrote:

'He actually swore that he met ten or twelve of us on the road, and that we demanded his arms, and he in return to our demand, presented his pistol at us, and said he would give us the contents of it before he would do so. In the name of common sense what would tempt this coxcomb to swear to such a notorious lie as this to frighten and face ten or twelve armed men. He is worthy of being classed with Sir William Wallace. I am astonished that after such a feat he did not petition the officer of the Hussars to fight the whole of us on the moor himself. But he had done enough for one day. But the truth of the matter is this – we never saw him on the road at all.'

On receiving Baird's report Lt. Hodgson decided to set out in pursuit of the Radicals, much to the dismay and grumbling of his soldiers who had just made a twelve hour ride from their base in Perth. It is significant how the soldiers happened to be in Kilsyth. The previous day they had received orders to travel to Stirling and be in readiness to ride to the Carron Iron Works, a clear indication the planned assault on Carron was known to the authorities. It was revealed later that a troop of the 80th Regiment of Foot were already inside the Carron works awaiting an attack. Hodgson's orders were then changed and he was told to ride on to Kilsyth. Not only were his men exhausted on arrival so also were their horses. Hodgson borrowed sixteen fresh horses from the Kilsyth Yeomanry, and Davidson supplied around the same number of the Kilsyth Yeomanry and they set out towards Falkirk in pursuit.

Meanwhile, just over a mile past Bonnybridge the two parties of Radicals had rejoined forces along with King. He told them he had been to Camelon and a large number of men from there would join them shortly. He suggested they get off the highway and rest on the moor and he would direct the Camelon men to them. King was never seen again. It is assumed that rather than going on to Camelon he rode to Kilsyth to brief Hodgson, as the soldiers had no difficulty in locating exactly the position of the Radicals on the moor.

The most reliable account of the unequal clash that took place there was supplied by Andrew Hardie, himself, which was written in his Stirling prison cell a few days before his execution.

'We went up about a mile into the moor and sat down at the top of a hill, and rested, I think, about an hour, when the cavalry made their appearance. Upon this we started to our feet, and at once resolved to meet them. I proposed to form into a square where we were, but Mr. Baird said it would be much better to go under cover of a dyke, which was not far distant. We then immediately ran down the hill cheering, and took up our position. There was a slap in the dyke which we filled with pikemen. The cavalry took a circular course through the moor and came under the cover of a wood at our right flank. As soon as they made their appearance past the end of the wood, firing commenced immediately. I cannot say who commenced firing first. I think the cavalry had fired a shot or two before they came to the wood, with the intention, probably, to frighten us, for they afterwards told us they did not expect us to face them. However, this is a matter of no importance. They came up nigh to the dyke, the Hussars in front, led by their officer, who called out to us to lay down our arms, but this was not agreed to. After firing shots at us, they made an attack at the slap, and got through, but were repulsed and driven back; they, in general, stood a little distance from the dyke, so that our pikes were rendered unserviceable. One of the Hussars came close up to the dyke, a little to the right of where I stood, and one of our party made a stab at him. The Hussar fired at us in turn, and he fell forward on his face. They made a second attack at the slap, and got through, but they were kept at bay in the inside, and the officer again called out to us to surrender, and he would do us no harm, which most of our men took for granted, and threw down their arms and ran. It will be here necessary to observe that some of our men never came into action at all, but made their way into a wood at some distance. But those who tried to make their escape after our surrender (viz, after the officer called out the second time, and by this time was in the inside of our side of the dyke) were instantly pursued, but were not all taken, and some of them wounded in a most shocking manner; and it was truly unbecoming the character of a British soldier to wound, or try to kill any man whom he had it in his power to take prisoner, and when they had no arms to make any defence. One of the Kilsyth Yeomanry was so inhuman, after he had sabred one of the men, sufficient as he thought to deprive him of life, as to try to trample him under his horse's feet; but here, my friends, the horse had more humanity than his master, and would not do as he wished him, but jumped over him, in place of trampling upon his wounded and mangled body; and after he returned from doing so, he called out (speaking very broad) 'that he had left him lying wi' his head cloven like a pot.' There were several others wounded.

'Mr. Baird defended himself in a most gallant manner; after discharging his piece he presented it at the officer empty, and told him he would do for him if he did not stand off. The officer presented his pistol at him, but it flashed and did not go off. Mr. Baird then took the butt of his piece and struck a private on the left thigh, whereupon the sergeant of the Hussars fired at him. Mr Baird then threw his musket from him and seized a pike, and while the sergeant was in the act of drawing his sword, wounded him in the right arm and side. Before this the officer was wounded on the right hand, and his horse was also wounded, yet, notwithstanding, he would not allow one of his men to do us any harm, and actually kept off with his own sword some of the strokes that were aimed against us. One of the Hussars recognised one of our party who (he said) had wounded his officer, and would have instantly sabred him had not the officer speedily interfered and told him there was too much done already. Although my enemy, I do him nothing but justice by saying that he is a brave and generous man. He came up in front of his men, and I am truly happy, but surprised, that he was not killed, as I know there were several shots fixed at him.' (The officer he was referring to was the commander of the operation Lt. Hodgson.)

The Democrats were rounded up, the wounded put on a borrowed cart, and the others marched to Stirling. The weapons of the Radicals were collected and taken to Stirling; they consisted of only five muskets, two pistols and eighteen pikes with a hundred pounds of ball cartridges. When formalities were completed at Stirling John Baird stepped forward and addressed the commanding officer.

'Sir, if there is to be any severity exercised towards us, let it be on me,' he said. 'I am their leader, and have caused them being here. I hope that I alone will suffer.' John Baird never resiled from that statement though he would have known it would cost him his life.

Meantime, a drama was still being played out at Bonnymuir. A Glasgow printer named Black who had fled from the scene was pursued by three members of the Kilsyth Yeomanry. One cried out, 'cut the

Radical bastard down.' Another struck out at him with a sabre inflicting serious wounds to his head and shoulders, and then they rode off leaving him for dead. But fortunately the whole event had been witnessed by farmer Alexander Robertson as he worked in his field. (3)

When the soldiers left, Robertson dragged Black back to his farmhouse, put him to bed, dressed his wounds and summoned a sympathetic doctor. But the military had been informed of Black's location. However, when they called to arrest him the doctor refused permission for him to be moved as he was in a critical condition. Eventually, the soldiers decided they would return for him the following day. Black, however, had an uncle, James MacClymont, a Larbert weaver. Robertson rode over to Larbert that evening to inform him of the situation, and during the night MacClymont and his son called at the farmhouse. Black made his escape out a back window wearing Robertson's blue bonnet as a disguise, and he was taken to Larbert. It was not long before the military were informed of his escape and a company of the local Yeomanry descended on MacClymont's home, but they were too late. He had been moved again. After several days avoiding the military Black was smuggled out of the country to safety.

But more dark deeds were to take place on the day of the Bonnymuir debacle. Later that night, around midnight, William Gardner was ordered to sound his bugle in Kilsyth. He was not told the reason but it soon became apparent when the Kilsyth Yeomanry assembled at the Kilsyth Cross.

The stillness of the night was disturbed 'with the sound of doors opening and shutting' as people enquired to what was going on. They were soon to find out. The din grew louder as more soldiers appeared, entered houses and dragged out targeted occupants. (4)

We have an insight into the thinking of the military. At 4 pm that afternoon, only a few hours after the events at Bonnymuir, Captain Nicholson who was in command of the troops at Falkirk, sent a dispatch to his senior officer. He suggested:

'I do think that now that blood has been shed and the business

begun by the Radicals themselves that here (Falkirk) and at
Camelon and St. Ninians, for the principal blackguards and
most notorious characters should at least be taken up. I am sure
what I have seen today that it would have an excellent effect to
take-up at least six fellows here (Falkirk) and as many at
Camelon, no matter whether anything eventually be actually
proved. The fright of being taken to Stirling Castle should have
great effect.'

In other words it was time for military terror.

We do not know how many were arrested in Kilsyth that night
but we are told that 'many honest people were carried away to prison,
that had no hand in the Bonnymuir incident. One of them was Robert
Gardner, ironically the father of William who had been ordered to
summon the Yeomanry. The Gardner family lived in the Main Street,
two houses from the Kilsyth Cross, and at that time Robert managed
the Black Bull tavern in the town. He was taken from his home and
family and plunged into the rat infested unspeakable conditions in
the dungeons of Stirling Castle. There he languished for nine weeks
under the threat of trial for sedition with the possibility of execution
or transportation. Archibald Gardner, his younger son who was only
five years old at the time, vividly recalled over forty years later his
mother taking him by the hand across to the Burngreen to welcome
his father home.

Robert Gardner was a clever and enterprising man; a skilled
carpenter, he managed taverns and grocery shops, he leased and
managed the mill which still stands on the Tak-Ma-Doon Road, and
also ran a small farm.

He was also a Democrat but committed to lawful and constitutional means. He organised meetings at the Black Bull and at his home,
as he was entitled to do. Why then was this man targeted by the
military? The answer is that previously, he had the audacity not only
to raise a law suit against the Edmonstone factor but went on to win
his case in court. Archibald Gardner later explained. 'The factor's
great pride was hurt, and he wreaked his vengeance on my father by
informing that he was a rebel.'

Robert had often talked of taking his family to America to build a new life. On his release he told his wife 'he would go to America even if he had to turn sailor and work his passage, before he would stay to be dragged from his home, and on the basis of spite, be imprisoned without redress.' He would go where he would enjoy liberty, he said.

As it turned out within seven weeks Robert and his family were on a list of six thousand people from the Glasgow area applying to emigrate to Canada. It was a familiar pattern as year after year Scotland was drained of its greatest asset, its people, as the most capable, enterprising and principled citizens were forced abroad to Scotland's loss and America's gain. The Gardner family were not unique in their success that followed. The family settled in Eastern Ontario and later moved to Utah in the United States.

Young Archibald, under the direction of his father, built his first mill when he was 17 years old. He went on build thirty-six gristmills and lumber mills besides hundreds of miles of canals and many bridges. The family prospered and lived out in full measure the American dream.

But to return to that fateful day, when news of events at Bonnymuir reached the cities newspapers reported fanciful accounts of how 100 heavily armed insurgents had been defeated, and church bells were sounded as if a great Imperial victory had been won. A dispatch rider bearing an equally fictitious account set off for London to report to Home Secretary Lord Sidmouth. On receiving the news Sidmouth personally took the news of the historic triumph to King George IV at Carlton House, and a special edition of the *London Gazette* was published giving a colourful account of the Government's great victory.

In the week following the Rising, the Tory *Glasgow Chronicle* observed, 'Kilsyth is noted for violent Radicals'. It went on to offer reassurance to its readers that the Kilsyth weavers were not about to bring the social order crashing down by adding 'but two troops of the 10th Hussars, besides the Yeomanry Cavalry, are at present doing duty in the village.' (5)

---

(1) Roach

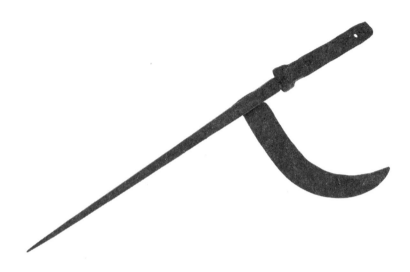

This is a Pike-Head made in Kilsyth for the planned insurrection known as the Pike Plot of 1794. It is one of two donated to the museum in 1841 by a Miss Wilson from Kilsyth. The label states 'Pike Heads – Friends of the People, Kilsyth'. This is misleading. Although the leaders of the Plot, Robert Watt and David Downie, had been members of the Friends of the People, the organisation was no longer operating. Indeed, at the time The Plot was devised Thomas Muir and the other leaders were on the high seas on their way to exile in Botany Bay. (National Museum of Scotland)

---

(2) Matthew Stevenson to William Kerr 3rd April 1820 Scottish Archives RH 2-4/132

(3) A more detailed account of the Battle of Bonnymuir can be found in *The Scottish Insurrection of 1820* by P. Berresford & Seumas Mac A' Ghobhainn

(4) Archibald Gardner Journal (Special Collections at the Brigham Young University Library, Provo, Utah) Researched by his direct descendent Jill N. Crandell

(5) *Glasgow Chronicle* (April 6th 1820)

CHAPTER 14

The messenger sent by the spy Turner to raise the Strathaven weavers did not arrive until Wednesday evening. Though the Strathaven men were not to know it, by that time the events at Bonnymuir were over. Their leaders immediately consulted James 'Perley' Wilson, a father figure of the Reform movement, who was 63 years old, a venerable age at that time. Wilson was a clever and talented weaver who had acquired the middle name Perley after he invented the stocking frame on which 'pearl stitches' could be worked. A free thinker he had been prominent in the Reform movement going back to the 1790s when he was a delegate at the first convention of the Friends of the People. He knew personally, and communicated with, all the great Reform campaigners.

Wilson immediately sent off a messenger to Glasgow saying the Strathaven men would be there by break of dawn. He told waverers that 'liberty was not worth having, if it is not worth fighting for'. During the night they prepared their weapons but by dawn only twenty-five volunteers had turned up. Nevertheless, the brave party set out on a fifteen mile march to Glasgow under their banner 'Scotland Free – or a Desert'. But around half way into their journey, information received convinced Wilson they had been betrayed. He pleaded with his colleagues to turn back but they refused. Wilson rested at the home of a friend before walking home to Strathaven.

When his colleagues reached Cathkin they found that Wilson had been right, and the area was deserted with no sign of the 5,000 men they were to join. The party knowing they were in mortal danger, hid their weapons and dispersed. That night James Wilson was arrested at his home, along with twelve colleagues who were apprehended on their way home.

With the collapse of the Insurrection the expected frenzy of repression began. Hundreds of prominent democrats were pursued and arrested, and Glasgow manufactures and merchants demanded that the Lord Provost convene a meeting to organise the withdrawal of work from anyone with radical associations. The plight of such action on innocent wives and children was, of course, not a consideration. From Established Church pulpits tirades of abuse were launched against the radicals over 'the great and bloody battle at Bonnymuir'.

The resistance, however, was not quite over. On Saturday of that eventful week five radical prisoners were moved from the overcrowded Paisley Prison to Greenock. As the drum beating troop of 80 soldiers entered Greenock they were greeted with jeers and taunts. After delivering the prisoners the military were jeered further, and stones and other missiles were thrown. The soldiers were ordered to fire over the heads of the crowd, but two people fell wounded and the angry crowd stepped up their protest. The soldiers then lost control and fired indiscriminately into the crowd. Three people died instantly, including 8 year-old James MacGilp; eighteen were seriously wounded, and six of them were to die from their wounds later.

The furious crowd, led by a piper, then marched on Greenock Prison, smashed down the wooden prison gates and released the five political prisoners. Only one of them was recaptured months later. This incident surprised everyone. As one historian put it, 'Unlike Paisley and Kilsyth there had been little reform action in Greenock.' However, it was not the last act of bloodshed in the town. A few months later soldiers 'maddened with drink' fired into another civilian crowd killing several people.

Across central and south Scotland no fewer than eighty-eight democrats were charged with High Treason, though many of them had fled abroad to avoid arrest. There was no doubt in any quarter that the familiar pattern of repression would follow; some highly publicised trials and executions designed to frighten the population, followed by a number of transportations. The rulers had learned nothing and forgotten nothing. Remembering the humiliation of the Andrew MacKinlay trial, Sidmouth ordered that the trials be conducted under English law. He further enraged defence lawyers by appointing a top English barrister, Mr Sergeant Hullock, to the prosecution team. Under the Treaty of Union no English lawyer could practise in a Scottish court unless he had a Scottish law degree, and no Scottish advocate could practise in an English court without an English law degree, a law which still applies today. Defence objections, however, were over-ruled.

The trials for High Treason began at Stirling on Thursday 13th July, and Andrew Hardie was first in the dock charged on four accounts of High Treason. The principal prosecution witnesses were the infamous Nicol Hugh Baird and the Glasgow Justice of the Peace, also named Hardie whom he had confronted over the removal of the proclamation. The Justice had given a grossly embellished account of the incident. Several of the Kilsyth Yeomanry gave evidence, including Alexander Coutts, a gardener at Colzium and John Rennie, a private with the Kilsyth Yeomanry. The trial went on until 2am the following morning when, after ten minutes deliberation, the jury returned a verdict of guilty.

When the court resumed later that morning John Baird was in the dock, and the evidence was similar to that given the previous day. At fifteen minutes past midnight the jury retired and when they returned two hours later they delivered a verdict of guilty. On the advice of Jeffrey, their advocate, the remaining sixteen Bonnymuir prisoners changed their plea to guilty, and the court was adjourned till 13th July for sentence.

The following week James Wilson's trial began in Glasgow. It lasted one day and Wilson was found guilty, but surprisingly the carefully selected jury of businessmen and members of the Yeomanry unanimously recommended Wilson to the mercy of the Crown. No mercy, however, could be expected from that quarter. The curt reply to the Jury's recommendation was that Wilson and his colleagues were not 'fit objects for Royal Mercy'. When Wilson appeared for sentence on Monday 24th July the judge asked him 'why the court should not give you judgment to die?' Composed and dignified, Wilson addressed the court:

'My lords and gentlemen, I will not attempt the mockery of a defence. Your are about to condemn me for attempting to overthrow the oppressors of my country. You do not know, neither can you appreciate, my motives. I commit my sacred cause, which is that of freedom, to the vindication of posterity. You may condemn me to immolation on the scaffold, but you cannot degrade me. If I have appeared as a pioneer in the van of freedom's battles – if I have attempted to free my country from political degradation – my conscience tells me I have done my duty. Your brief authority will soon cease, but the vindictive proceedings this day shall be recorded in history. The principles for which I have contended are as immutable, as imperishable, as the eternal laws of nature. My gory head may in a few days fall on the scaffold and be exposed as the head of a traitor, but I appeal with confidence to posterity. When my countrymen have exalted their voices in bold proclamation of the rights and dignity of Humanity, and enforced their claim by the extermination of their oppressors, then, and not till then, will some future historian do my memory justice, then will my name and sufferings be recorded in Scottish history – then will my motives be understood and appreciated; and with the confidence of an honest man, I appeal to posterity for that justice which in all ages and in all countries been awarded to those who have suffered martyrdom in the glorious cause of liberty.'

Lord Hope warned the newspapers to use discretion in what they reported. The *Glasgow Herald* duly complied. It reported that Wilson 'stammered out a few words in an incoherent manner'. After a short speech the judge went on: 'The sentence of the law is – that you be drawn on a hurdle to the place of execution, on the 30th August, and after being hung by the neck till you are dead, that your head be severed from your body, and your body cut in quarters, to be at the disposal of the King; and the Lord have mercy on your soul.'

Wilson replied: 'I am not deceived. You might have condemned me without this mummery of a trial. You want a victim; I will not shrink from the sacrifice. I have neither expected justice nor mercy here. I have done my duty to my country. I have grappled with her oppressors for the last forty years and having no desire to live in slavery, I am ready to lay down my life in support of these principles which must ultimately triumph.'

When the Bonnymuir prisoners appeared for sentence on 24th August all eighteen were sentenced to death along with four colleagues from the Falkirk area. The judge made clear that Baird and Hardie were the principal targets. He said: '. . . it is utterly impossible to suppose, considering the convulsions into which this country was thrown, that the Crown must not feel a necessity of making some terrible example, and as you were the leaders, I am afraid that example must be given by you.'

In Kilsyth and elsewhere these events were followed closely, and their must have been a depressing view that the Democratic movement had been irretrievably crushed; but in the long struggle for human justice the greater the repression the more recruits are inspired to pick up the baton and face down the threat of martyrdom.

One consequence the purblind Government had not taken into account was that these Democrats were presented to the world in a very different light. They had been widely portrayed as ignorant, uncouth, blood-thirsty villains, but by their deportment through the trial, their writings in prison and the dignity and courage with which they faced execution, a very different picture emerged. Not only were they erudite, eloquent and principled, but committed and devout Christians, as dignified and generous as they were brave. Their notes and letters smuggled out of their death cells were circulated and later published, adding to the legend. For this, posterity has to thank 'Granny' Duncan, who lived off the Esplanade at Stirling and who attended Baird and Hardie through their last days. One ingenious subterfuge she employed was to make porridge for the prisoners; she would allow it to set, remove the porridge from the pot and place the correspondence underneath.

Both Baird and Hardie had asked Daniel Taylor of Kilsyth, a close friend of John Baird, to write their memorial. In a letter to Daniel Taylor John Baird wrote:

Dear Friend,

I take this opportunity of sending you my long and last farewell.
On Friday I am to be made immortal. Although man may
mangle this body, yet blessed be God, he had kept the most
noble part in his own hand. I do not mean to say anything about
them who have been so sore against me, for I have made it my
study to forget and forgive all men any wrong that they have
done to me. I received your kind and welcome letter. It cheered
my very heart to think you will go so far to see my grave; and it
gave me some consolation to hear you say, you will write my
dirge. All this, you have said, I hope you will do. It gives me no
small concern to think that any person blames you concerning
me; that I never could do; I look on you still as my trusty friend;
but you know men are oft blamed, when they are not worthy of
it. I hope you will let all animosity cease, and let love and
harmony abound, is the sincere wish of your dying friend.

Let troubles rise and tyrants rage,
And days of darkness fall;
But those who wait upon the Lord,
Shall more than conquer all.

'If God be for us, who can stand against us?' 'It is God that
justifieth, who is he that can condemn?' No more from your
dying friend, a martyr to the cause of liberty. May the grace of
God protect you and yours. Give my kind love to all friends of
liberty.
John Baird

Andrew Hardie wrote in the same letter,

Dear Sir,

This comes from a hand you never saw, to the best of my
knowledge – from a hand that in a few days must mingle with
its native dust. Hard is our fate, my dear unknown friend; yet, I
resign my life without the least reluctance, knowing that it is
for the cause of truth and justice; and to which I remain under

conviction. I die a martyr –

'I die firm to the cause, like a magnet to its pole,
With undaunted spirit and unshaken soul.'

My dear friend I must bid you farewell; and I hope you will
keep in remembrance the cause for which Baird, Hardie and
Cleland died on the scaffold. No more, farewell.
I am, sir, your most obedient servant,
Andrew Hardie.
PS Since writing this, I am happy to announce that Clelland has
got a respite.

In fact it was only three days before he was to mount the scaffold
that James Clelland, who like Baird and Hardie was a former soldier,
joined the other Bonnymuir prisoners in having his sentence
commuted to transportation.

Hardie's letters, like Baird's, were pervaded by Biblical quotes
and references. He also extended Christian forgiveness to his
persecutors. In a letter to his relatives he wrote:

'. . . If I can't forgive my enemies, or those that have injured me,
how can I expect my blessed Saviour to make intercession for
me? Who so freely forgave his, even when expiring on the cross
he prayed for his enemies: 'Father forgive them, they know not
what they do'. I could take the greatest enemy that I have into
my bosom, even the perjured Baird, who, in the presence of
Almighty God, and a large assembly, stained and imbrued his
hands in my innocent blood; even also the unrelenting Hardie
(The Glasgow Justice of the Peace who gave false evidence
against him) who voluntarily came to prove my ruin. Yes, my
friends, my earnest prayer to God, is that he may forgive them
. . . I hope you will keep no ill-will to them, and as my prayers
on this earth will soon be ended, I earnestly beg of you to mind
them in yours.'

In a moving letter he bid farewell to Margaret MacKeigh the girl he planned to marry. He concluded by asking her to visit frequently his 'distressed and afflicted mother'. . . 'At the expense of some tears I destroyed your letters. Again, farewell my dear Margaret, may God attend you still, and all your soul with consolation fill, is the sincere prayer of your most affectionate and constant lover while on earth.' (1)

Public executions of the time were grizzly affairs, half circus and half horror show, with stalls, entertainment and a fair-day atmosphere. But that was not the scene on that bright summer day of the 30th August 1820 when James Wilson paid the ultimate price for freedom and democracy. More troops than had ever before attended an execution were brought into Glasgow to watch over the 20,000 solemn and silent crowd. Hand bills circulated among the crowd declared, 'May the ghost of the butchered Wilson, haunt the pillows of his relentless jurors – Murder! Murder! Murder!'

After a religious service in the County Court building in which Wilson joined in singing the psalms the prisoner was placed in a hurdle along with his masked executioner who carried a large headsman's axe in one hand and a knife in the other. Throughout, James Wilson was the most composed and serene person present. After ascending the scaffold, which had been erected near the River Clyde, the rope was fixed around his neck, and when he dropped his handkerchief to indicate he was ready to die the trap door was sprung. The body hung for half an hour then it was laid down and the executioner severed James Wilson's head with one stroke of the axe. He then picked up the severed head saying, 'This is the head of a traitor'.

Several soldiers fainted at the sight and the crowd shouted in protest, 'He is a murdered man' and 'He bled for his country.' The body was then taken to a pauper's grave near Glasgow High Church and buried without ceremony. This came as a shock to the family who were standing by to take the body back to Strathaven for burial in keeping with Wilson's dying wish. The family, however, were not to meekly accept this last act of cruelty. At midnight Wilson's daughter and his niece, along with a few helpers, went to the grave, dug-up the coffin and transported it back to Strathaven where it was secretly re-buried a few yards from James Wilson's house. The authorities were furious but decided against taking any action against the family and local minister.

Eight days later the second phase of the plan designed to crush democracy for ever was duly enacted. Baird and Hardie spent their last night on Earth in Stirling Castle in prayer and conversation with ministers and friends. They had two hours' sleep and after morning prayers were allowed into the castle's courtyard to say farewell to their colleagues. They told them that 'although they were condemned, right was on their side and the cause which they championed would in the end prevail.'

After warmly embracing their friends they were led back to their cells to await the procession to the scaffold which had been erected in Broad Street, in front of Stirling Jail. As the procession of soldiers, sheriff and magistrates set off Baird and Hardie, who had been placed in a hurdle with their executioner, clutched a Bible in their hands and sang the hymn 'The Hour of My departure Comes'. On arrival they were escorted into the court hall for a religious service, and from there to the scaffold.

John Baird stepped forward and addressed the crowd.

> 'Friends and countrymen, I dare say you will expect me to say something to you of the cause which has brought me here; but on that I do not mean to say much, only that what I have hitherto done, and which brought me here, was for the cause of truth and justice. I declare I never gave my consent to anything inconsistent with truth and justice.'

He told the silent crowd he was not afraid to confront God and he exhorted the crowd to believe in God, to love and venerate the Bible. Hardie expressed similar sentiments and ended by saying,, 'I die a martyr to the cause of truth and justice.' The crowd who had been solemn and grave gave a roar of applause and the nervous soldiers were ordered to 'present arms'. When calm was restored the execution cap was placed on the heads of the two men and they bade farewell to each other. The noose was tightened around their necks, and when Hardie gave the signal both men died without a struggle.

As the executioner moved forward with his axe to behead them the crowd shouted in protest and cried 'Murderer!' and the soldiers were again ordered to 'present arms'. And so Baird and Hardie left this world and the legend which was to inspire many others to join the struggle for democracy was born.

Francis Jeffrey, who was later to become a High Court judge, wrote to a friend:

> 'I am very much ashamed of the Commons, and have little now to say against the Radical Reformers; if any reform is worth the risk of such an experiment. The practical question upon which every man should be making up his mind is, whether he is for tyranny or revolution.'

Daniel Taylor kept his promise and travelled from Kilsyth to Stirling and at the graveside read his seventeen verse 'The Dirge to Baird and Hardie.' It ended:

> Though near this place no marble statute stand,
> Nor weeping angel pointing to the spot,
> Their fame is know all through their native land,
> And never, never, shall they be forgot.

In 1847 the Scottish Chartists, who had taken up the struggle for democracy, petitioned the Government to have the remains of Baird and Hardie removed to Sighthill Cemetery in Glasgow. In the early hours of July 20th. the exhumations were carried out under the strict conditions laid down by the Government and re-interred under a large handsome monument which read:

Erected by Public Subscription
July 1847
To the memory of
John Baird, aged 32
And
Andrew Hardie, age 28
Who for the Cause of Freedom, suffered Death
At Stirling, 8th September, 1820

The small village of Condorrat lost four of its brave democrats: John Baird, Thomas McFarlane, John Barr and William Smith. In the years that followed the British public became better informed of the true events attending the Scottish Insurrection and the role and dark deeds of the Government and its agents. They were equally engrossed and repelled by the revelations in the court case in London when the spy, Richmond, attempted to sue the publisher of Peter MacKenzie's revelations. The case was laughed out of court but the damage to the Government's reputation had been done.

In 1835 the King granted an absolute pardon to the surviving Bonnymuir prisoners but most of them chose not to return to 'the land of the free'. One who did was Thomas McFarlane. Although he had been born in Strathaven it is likely that his wife, Elizabeth Baird, was a Kilsythian. The couple had spent the early years of their marriage in Kilsyth, and three of their seven children were born there. It is believed that Elizabeth died before Thomas returned, but the census of 1841 established that Thomas was back living in Condorrat at the home of his son. William Smith's wife, Levinia, may also have been a Kilsythian as she moved from Condorrat to Kilsyth after William was transported. She was said to be living in great distress but in 1822 she and her two daughters and two sons were allowed to join William in Australia where it was reported that the family lived successful lives. (2)

In Chapter 11 we considered the differences between modern historians. One other charge that was levelled at the authors of the *Scottish Insurrection 1820* by other historians of the period was that they lent credibility to the false theory that the Scottish democrats were let down by their English colleagues. The theory does not take account of the fact that on April 1st, the planned day of the Rising, 2,000 Democrats made an attempt to take over Huddersfield. Four were arrested with two being transported and the others imprisoned for two years.

After the Rising in England was adjourned to 12th April four hundred democrats from Barnsley and Grange Moor assembled for an attack on Huddersfield. On the same day a 'group of well drilled men' gathered to attack the military barracks at Sheffield. Three hundred armed men assembled at Wigan, and two hundred at Carlisle in answer to the call from Scotland. There were also simultaneous strikes at Sheffield, Dewsbury and Mirfield. Why all these efforts failed is not clear. It may have been the difficulty in communication at the time or, like the Scottish movement, the English democrats had been heavily infiltrated by spies, or perhaps a combination of both. One point is certain, although many English democrats were transported and imprisoned the treatment meted out by the English courts was not nearly as savage as the sentences imposed in Scotland.

But after such a disastrous interlude even the greatest optimist could not have foreseen the dramatic events that would take place before the decade was out

---

(1) The letters of Baird and Hardie are contained in *The Scottish Insurrection of 1820* P. Berresford & Seumas Mac A' Ghobhainn (Victor Gollancz Ltd. 1970)
(2) MacFarlane, Margaret and Alastair *The Scottish Radicals* (SPA Books 1981)

CHAPTER 15

EVEN AS THE TRAGIC END to the Scottish Insurrection was being played out, an upturn in the economy was underway. It was to be the first sustained boom in the cotton industry since the Napoleonic War and was to build up until the high point of 1825. No doubt the Kilsyth weavers, like others, were taking all the work they could handle to pay off debts and, if possible, accumulate some savings. The political climate also changed significantly. By 1822 Castlereagh and Sidmouth had departed office; Castlereagh committed suicide by cutting his own throat with a pen knife. The iconoclastic Lord Byron marked his passing by penning a short inelegant verse.

> Posterity will ne'er survey
> a nobler grave than this:
> Here lie the bones of Castlereagh:
> Stop, traveller, and piss.

Castlereagh was replaced by the more liberal George Canning and repression and censorship eased. But this new dispensation made possible what the more perceptive of the ruling landowning class feared most of all – an alliance of the middle and working classes. The middle class had always been resentful of a Government which was corrupt and indifferent to their interests, but while there was agitation on the streets they were more concerned with perceived danger to their property than fighting for democracy.

One man more than any other brought about this unity of the classes – Thomas Attwood, a Birmingham banker and brilliant economist whose ideas on how a modern economy should be managed, in many respects, pre-dated by a century the insights of John Maynard Keynes. He described the House of Commons as a seat of 'ignorance, imbecility and indifference'. Later, after he became the first MP for Birmingham, he was asked if he stuck to that opinion. 'Not at all,' he replied, he now realised it was much worse than that.

In the second half of the 1820s pressure for reform grew steadily. In June 1830 the despotic King George IV died to be replaced by King William IV and expectations soared further as the new King was said to be in favour of reform, although he was soon to revert to type. The death of King George necessitated a General Election which the Tories won, but under the fierce anti-reformer the Duke of Wellington, they were hopelessly divided. Within weeks the Government fell and with no Tory administration available Charles Grey, now Lord Grey, and leader of the Whigs, became Prime Minister.

The Whigs, who had been out of power for almost twenty-five years, regarded some measure of reform as inevitable and now was their chance to control it and get back in power. They recognised that many opponents of reform were changing sides in fear of something worse. The clinching issue for some was what became known as the 'Swing Riots' when agricultural labourers in Kent began to burn hayricks. It was feared that if such a normally subservient class of men were prepared to go to such lengths, the complete fabric of society was at risk.

It is not necessary to go through all the political machinations of the period but when Lord Grey presented the first Reform Bill in March 1831 it was savaged in the Commons. He immediately called for the dissolution of Parliament and took the issue to the country and the Whigs won the subsequent election with an overwhelming majority. In September the second Reform Bill got through the Commons with a majority of 100, but when it went to the House of Lords it was thrown out by 41 votes. The outcome was an outburst of serious violence in many parts of the country and Britain was never closer to revolution.

At the start of the new session of Parliament, after making a number of compromises, Grey presented his third Reform Bill which was passed in the Commons with an even larger majority. However, the Lords blocked its progress creating what seemed an impossible impasse. Grey's solution was for the King to create a batch of new peers to get the legislation through, but although there was a precedent for such action, the King refused. Grey resigned and the King invited the Duke of Wellington to return and form a Government. He tried, but failed, and the King had no option but to bring Grey back and agree to his terms. At this point the Lords were defeated and the anti-reformers absented themselves when the vote went through. On June 7th 1832 the Royal assent was given and the Great Reform Act became law with Acts for Scotland and Ireland to follow.

The new Act, however, fell far short of a universal franchise. Only one Scottish male in eight had the vote, and that did not include the Kilsyth weavers who fell short of the property qualification. Yet, their joy was boundless. Robert Anderson was only eight years old but writing some seventy years later he recalled the celebrations as if it was yesterday.

'Two months after the passing of the Bill it was resolved to have a meeting of the newly empowered electors from Kilsyth, Kirkintilloch, Campsie and Balfron, to be held at Inchbelly, about four miles west of Kilsyth, and central for the other districts. The Kilsyth party, before setting out, met in the Relief Church. My father was asked to address them, which he did. They sang the 20th Psalm and the 5th verse —'In Thy salvation we will joy; in our God's name we will lift up our banners,' etc. At Inchbelly there was an immense concourse. Among others on the platform were Admiral the Honourable Charles E. Fleming, and his young son, who both addressed the throng, and the youth called forth the remark about the old cock and the young in the matter of 'crawing'. I was only eight years old, but I was there in the procession. Old flags that had waved over the news of Camperdown, the Nile, Trafalgar, Vemeira, Vittoria and Waterloo, were brought out, new ones were made, and, headed by the brass band, with William Fife at the big drum, Bugler Sinclair and the rest of them, nearly the whole town was marching away. My two older brothers were there as well as myself, and we had a flag of our own making, and a device and motto of our own contriving. There was a whip on it, for the

Tories, surrounded by the words, 'Though young in years, yet strong in Reform'. The miners, then a young industry, declared on their flag, 'We have come from the bowels of the earth to claim our rights.' The weavers, who were on the front, had something about 'the loom of time weaving the web of progress'. The enthusiasm kept up all the four miles of trampling, and when the speakers told us it had cost our forefathers sixty years of cruel suffering to gain this victory, which was the dawn of future progress, thousands of throats gave echo to the fact and hurrahed till they were hoarse.'

Four of the banners made for those halcyon days were found in 1957 when John Smith was clearing out his attic at 4 Church Lane. They are now in the Summerlee Museum of Scottish Industrial Life at Coatbridge (see back cover). They read:

KILSYTH WEAVERS – WE'RE HERE, AWAY FROM
LOOM AND SHUTTLE TO FORCE THE LORDS THEIR
HOUSE TO SKUTTLE:

KILSYTH MINERS – WE COME FROM THE BOWELS OF
THE EARTH TO DEMAND OUR RIGHTS

THE FRANCHISE BILL
(Portrait of Gladstone)
THE PEOPLE'S BILL

KILSYTH FOUR POUNDERS – READY FOR ACTION
THE HOUSE OF LORDS MUST BE ENDED.

The 'Four Pounders', requires some explanation. When the reforming Whig Government took power a ministerial committee was set up to prepare measures of reform. One of its proposals was to set a standard qualification for voters at the high level of property worth at least £20 a year. Lord Grey was aware that would exclude too many aspiring voters to satisfy public demand, and on his urging it was lowered to £10. This however, still excluded working men, including the Kilsyth weavers. The 'Four Pounders' was a demand to have the qualifying figure for the franchise reduced to £4.

There is some dubiety regarding the origin of the Four Pounders banner at the Summerlee Museum. Was it made for the 1832 celebrations or for a later campaign to extend democracy? If it was an 1832 banner it would suggest that the Kilsyth weavers had not only anticipated the next battleground for Democracy, but had already moved on to it.

Many researchers have attempted and failed to uncover who were the 'Four Pounders'. When the banners were found in 1957 Kilsyth Town Council even initiated enquires to shed light on the mystery. In my view, the reason they all failed was because the Four Pounders was not an organisation at all, but a slogan – and a mischievous, ambiguous and cleverly worded slogan at that. A 'Four Pounder' was a cannon in use at that time. The wording on the banner —'Kilsyth Four Pounders – Ready for Action' was, I suggest, deliberately given a military connotation to invest it with a double meaning.

But following the passing of the Reform Act the Tories did not sulk in their tents. Every ploy, legal and illegal, was engaged to frustrate the will of Parliament. An army of professional agents were employed in constituencies throughout the country to challenge the voting rights of everyone with liberal sympathies. Full use and abuse was made of what was known as the Chandos Amendment, which allowed the vote to tenant farmers. There being no secret vote it would have been a brave tenant who would vote against the will of his landlord. Voters who could not be persuaded to vote Tory were intimidated and those who could not be intimidated were bribed. Nowhere were underhand practices applied more vigorously than in Stirlingshire. The lairds of Garden and Leckie marched their tenants to the poll like sheep to vote for Forbes of Callendar. (1) Glasgow and Edinburgh Tories bought up old weaving shops, and even pigsties, in Kilsyth as the basis to create false documents to give their friends and family voting rights. (2)

A Kilsyth reformer wrote to the *Reformers Gazette* under the heading 'Strange What Money Does – Sir, A Town Clerk, not twelve miles from Glasgow, who was three months ago a great Whig – nay, even a Radical – would you believe it, is now canvassing for a Tory, – why? – because he is well paid for doing so'. The editor helpfully added a footnote. 'To be plain – does this allude to Mr. W.C. Wilson, Town Clerk of Kilsyth?'

Voters were required first of all to register to vote and then return on polling day to cast their votes. The Act stated that the place required for both should be the 'most accessible and convenient' for the voters. Balfron was the most populous town in west Stirlingshire and the most central location, but the sheriff chose the inaccessible hamlet of Drymen in the furthest extremity of the County, requiring prospective voters to walk up to fifteen miles to attend. Despite this ploy on the day the Registration Court was to meet a large number of people had made their way to Drymen, as the Tory agent had lodged objections to all whose votes they regarded as suspect. The sheriff, however, arrived many hours late, explaining he had been detained at a cattle show in Dumfries, and the court had to be adjourned to the following day. It was a ferociously stormy day and night, and many of the prospective voters had to spend a miserable night in local outhouses.

At nearby Killearn even more extreme measures were resorted to when the feudal Lord, or superior, John Blackburn, found a strong body of support for Admiral Fleming – he threatened to demolish their homes! Blackburn, who had made his fortune through slavery as a West Indian planter, found a clause in the tenants' title deeds which stated 'that no tenant shall erect more than one house on his tenement and that no more than one family shall reside in the house under penalty of forfeiting his lease'. Over the years a number of tenants had built extensions to their property with the approval and consent of Blackburn who was only too pleased to charge additional rent. In a letter to the tenants he stated:

> '. . . if more than one family reside in one house after the term of Martinmas, I shall enforce the penalty, and if any person has erected more houses than one, he must pull them down before that time.'

These were only a few of numerous shady deeds in efforts to fix that and following elections.

Not that the weavers in Kilsyth did not try to exert their own pressure. Robert Anderson recalled:

'For Kilsythians the polling place for this open voting was Campsie, and as crowds of Kilsyth folks went there to see how things got on, they who voted Tory had to suffer for it when they got home at night. The town was wild at them. Their windows were broken, their effigies, both lay and clerical, made to the life, were burned in the Market Place, or they were hung up by the neck from tree branches to be pelted to bits with stones. It was not safe for a Tory to be out of doors. I remember one being mobbed near the Cross Keys. He was tall and strong, and seizing the crutch of a cripple near him, he laid about vigorously, and escaped, bleeding, mud-smeared and hatless. A well known townsman, and a Tory, provoked beyond endurance by the damage done to his property, threw open his door and fired a pistol at the crowd. He got the door slammed to in time to save his life. At that time special constables were sworn in. One of them was the hero of the crutch. He was a big 'gomeril', but fearless. Flourishing his baton, he rushed at the crowd, shouting 'In the name of George Rex I dismiss this mob.' He was received with a roar of laughter, for George Rex had been awhile in his grave. A man, who had been a prominent Radical and had got a fine eight day clock from his admirers, turned his coat. He had actually voted Tory that day at Campsie. During the night his window was quietly lifted and the clock, pushed over with a stick, fell with a crash at his bedside.'

One advantage of the partial reform was that the principle of reform was now on the national agenda, and could not be dismissed as the seditious deeds of a rabble. Kilsyth's grandee, Sir Archibald Edmonstone, was to address no fewer than six extensive letters to the voters of Stirlingshire urging them to vote Tory. Even if the local weavers had access to those letters, and a forum to express their views, it would have been a brave soul who would confront such a powerful local figure. But there was one man who could, and did, take up the challenge. He was a remarkable neighbouring landowner, John McFarlan the laird of Ballencleroch. His family home was Ballencleroch House in Campsie Glen. It later became the luxury Campsie Glen Hotel which was burned down in the 1980s. The house was rebuilt and is now run as a shrine and retreat by the Schoenstatt Sisters of Mary. McFarlan's views published in four pamphlets, two of them at least directed at Edmonstone, merit more attention than they have received.

McFarlan was both a deeply committed Calvinist and in temper and intellect a man of the Enlightenment. One theme that has emerged in the course of this narrative, the strong connection between the struggle for the democratic liberties of the Church and the campaign for civil democracy – was identified by McFarlan 175 years ago.

There was no personal animosity between him and Edmonstone, but that did not cause him to pull his punches in denouncing the views of Edmonstone and his Tory friends. Forensically, he took apart their polices and record at home and abroad.

'As to religion,' he wrote, 'the leaders of that Party know nothing and care nothing.' He claimed if the Archbishop of Canterbury were to put them through the Shorter Catechism he would find it necessary to send the great majority to school. Despite his own strong Calvinist beliefs McFarlan made a plea for religious tolerance. He wrote: 'Every sect professes to appeal to Scripture as its authority, but each one has its own interpretation of the inspired volume; and amidst contending interpretations who shall decide which is false and which is true? To decide on such a subject, and in these circumstances, is presumptuous – to act upon such decision is bigotry.'

He claimed, 'there is not in the annuals of Christendom one instance of a nation, nay not one of an individual, converted by the iron hand of despotic authority.' He went on: 'In good truth, the more I love, the more I respect, the more I honour those from whom I differ, the more earnest I shall be in my efforts to convert them.'

McFarlan was particularly incensed by Edmonstone's opposition to universal education, which offended both his religious and political values. In this, McFarlan was holding true to the longstanding Presbyterian defence of education; if each person was to strike their own direct relationship with God it was necessary to read and interpret the Bible, and that required education. He went on to give detailed examples where the appeal of Christianity was enhanced, not diminished, by education.

In his pamphlet *Who Are The Friends Of Religion And the Church? – Being An Answer to Sir Archibald Edmonstone's Six Letters To the Electors of Stirlingshire* he wrote: 'Never let it be said that money devoted to elementary education, to the teaching of reading, is not devoted to the cause of religion.'

It is not surprising that McFarlan, despite his high social standing as a landowner and advocate, was a committed supporter of democracy and Thomas Muir. Like Muir, he remained within the Church of Scotland, though neither an uncritical nor a silent member. It was that rational Enlightenment strand of his thinking which made him critical of those ministers who did not engage properly with the atheist arguments of the great philosopher, David Hume. 'They did not honour it with attention enough to enable them to understand it.' The case for religion, he claimed, had been squandered by simplistic denunciations.

Although McFarlan's case against Edmonstone was meticulously argued on the basis of principle, evidence and reasoning, he had, as the Campsie based writer David McVey, points out, the ability to turn a phrase to polemical advantage. How is this for a broadside at his Tory opponents? He summed up their values as 'Down with the people and up with their masters – Down with liberty and equal law and up with unlimited lawless power – The more slavery, the less liberty, the better.'

He concluded: 'The grand problem with a Tory always is, not how much liberty a people is qualified to possess, and to enjoy, but how much servitude they may be able to endure.' The modern day spin doctor would have doffed his cap in recognition of a master of their craft.

But here we must confront a thorny question: Was the Great Reform Act a victory for the Democrats or for the Aristocracy? The answer is not as obvious as it may appear. The Whigs were not democrats but aristocratic, indeed it has been observed that Grey's Cabinet was the most blue blooded of the nineteenth century. (3) They were determined to keep government in the hands of the property owning class and enfranchising the middle class was the only way of doing so. It could be regarded as a classic example of surrendering power in order to retain it.

Should there be any doubt, Lord Grey, himself, spelt out his purpose in a speech to the House of Lords in 1831: 'The principle of my reform is to prevent the necessity for revolution... there is no one more dedicated against annual parliaments, universal suffrage, and the ballot, than I am.'

He made clear he would not abandon the principle of aristocratic government; rather the Whigs would strengthen it by attaching to the existing constitution the new forms of propertied interest. Grey's estimate turned out to be right. (4) By 1860 Government still remained firmly in the hands of the aristocratic land-owning class. The new battle line for the Whigs was to keep government firmly in the hands of property owning interest, which to a large extent was themselves. Karl Marx is reputed to have described the British aristocracy as 'the shrewdest in the world – they give half an inch a century.'

Yet, the Democrats had good cause to rejoice; as they were only too well aware the Rubicon had been crossed. Monarchical/Aristocratic government could no longer be claimed to be the divine order of things. Democracy was now a question of degree with the door being opened for further reform.

Of course it was a bitter sweet reaction in that those weavers, who had more than anyone contributed and sacrificed so much to bring reform about, were excluded from the vote. As Anderson reported, 'Those left out remained discontented Radicals, with wives angrier than themselves. All these complexities were well understood by the Kilsyth weavers. Indeed, John Kirkwood succinctly summed it all up in verse:

Ah! deem not the blessings of freedom are ours,
Though the laws of the nation seem kind;

Though the tree of corruption is swept of its flowers,
The poison still lurks in the rind.

Like the earliest shrubs of our dark frowning north,
'Twill awake in the first vernal beam,
'Twill steal into life and its blossoms put forth,
Then Reason shall scorn your esteem.

O, who like the monarch of England appeared,
While assuming the patriot's air?
The nations adored, till the hopes he had reared,
Were whelmed in the depth of despair.

Beware, then, my friend, be not caught with the glare,
Or the shades of a partial Reform;
Though intrigues from the first were designed to ensnare,
There is hope in the slow-charging storm.

It was that 'hope in the slow-charging storm' that gave the Democrats cause for unrestrained celebration, and not early changes in the conditions that afflicted them. The people in power remained in power and were to do so for many years. Seven years after the Great Reform Act, Government Commissioners investigating the conditions of handloom weavers found in the west of Scotland that 'they were poor and often inadequately fed, eating very little meat. The weavers usually slept in straw beds but some houses still had good furniture, a remainder of former prosperous times, as was the good education of the older weavers.' (5)

Nevertheless, they rejoiced and in doing so did not forget the heroes and martyrs who made the breakthrough possible.

After the provost of Stirling refused consent for the memory of Baird and Hardie to be honoured in the town of their execution, in November 1832 a handsome memorial was erected at Thrushgrove where in 1816 over 40,000 people gathered to launch the campaign for Democracy. It was followed by a dinner attended by 120 leading Reformers. Robert Baird, John's brother, proposed a toast to Admiral

Fleming, who had warned several Democrats of their impending arrest, allowing them time to flee the country.

When the Reform Bill was passed, a transparency was displayed in Glasgow illustrating the image of Thomas Muir as a central part of the City's celebrations. During three weeks of celebration a grand Jubilee took place in Edinburgh, organised by the Trades Union Council with all the crafts marching behind their banners. On the platform was an empty chair draped in black in memory of Muir. In Sheffield, Reformers sang songs in praise of the Scottish Martyrs. But the most poignant celebration was by Andrew Hardie's elderly mother who placed a card in her window:

> 'Britons rejoice, Reform is won!
> But twas the cause
> Lost me my son.'

(1) *The Reformers Gazette* (December 29th 1832)

(2) *Reformers Gazette* (June 30th)

(3) Evans, E.J. *The Great Reform Act 1832* Methuem London and New York

(4) Ibid

(5) Reports from Assistant Hand-Loom Weavers' Commissioners, Accounts and Papers 1839 Vol. XL11, 212p (Sessional no. 159)

CHAPTER 16

WE LEAVE the Kilsyth weavers at the high point of 1832. Not that they disappeared then from the scene, but because Kilsyth was embarking on a process of fundamental change. The decline of handloom weaving was to take place sporadically through the remainder of the century. One principal cause was the gradual triumph of the power loom, and as work and wages dropped the burgeoning Industrial Revolution was creating work in new sectors. In Kilsyth women found employment in small local handloom factories until they eventually closed. Nevertheless the craft survived into the early years of the twentieth century before breathing its last.

Anderson reported:

> '. . . there were still a few aged relics of the past, women chiefly, who, unable to earn a penny any other way, were supplied with webs by J&P Wilson. There they weaved on the looms of their youth, now worm eaten and frail. The picture is a pathetic one. There is an old weaver yet, and he is sitting in the deserted shop, once, as he minds it, so full of life and work and song. It is cold, the fire is out, and as he slowly drives his shuttle, there is a 'snell drap' at his nose. With him old Kilsyth passes away.'

But we should avoid the impression that the Great Reform Act brought any discernible improvement to the lives of the weavers. Indeed, in many respects life became harsher. While the British Empire spawned fortunes for some beyond the dreams of avarice, for the weavers and other working people life oscillated between hard times and desperate times.

It is helpful to remind ourselves of the break-neck pace of change.

Until the second half of the 1700s the day-to-day life under rural feudalism had gone on largely unchanged for centuries. Then came the first phase of the Industrial Revolution bringing such an abundance of independence, prosperity and hope. Yet, within one generation, the people were thrust into the horrors of the capitalist factory and coal mining systems where any remaining semblance of *noblesse oblige* was swept away, and millions were sacrificed at the altar of profit.

As Tom Johnston put it:

> 'No pen will ever paint even a dim picture of the horrors of the early years of the capitalist system in the factory towns. A plethora of labourers, cottars from the soil, handicraftsmen from the villages, driven to little, overcrowded, bleak and cheerless hovels, hastily erected around the factory walls; compelled to sell their toil in foul and filthy working conditions, and for the barest pittances; from dawn to sunset bullied and oppressed, the last ounce taken from their bodies by scarcely less oppressed overseers; hunger, misery, dirt; no sanitary or factory regulations; no machinery fenced; their children killed off like flies, and they themselves emaciated, consumptive, and without hope; no Trade Union or Friendly Society benefits; no co-operative societies; no holidays at the seaside; no part in citizenship; the only relaxation being on the Sabbath, when a clergyman, voicing the desires of his chief paymaster in the raised pew, would urge submission to the present Hell as a qualification for the Paradise to come.'

The early 1840s were a particularly dark time. Johnston recorded that the herring fishing failed, and there was depression everywhere from Lerwick to Dumfries, except, perhaps, among child labour, which, as at Kilsyth, 'was worked for 14 hours a day'.

Those Kilsyth children were employed in local coal mines; and we have their accounts of the conditions they endured, which are all the more powerful in that they come from the lips of the innocent.

William Marshall was 10 or 11 years old. He said:

'I draw father's coals. Have done so for twelve months. I wrought three years before with father at handloom weaving but it was no good, as father said 'the loom would na get us oatmeal'. Coal work is more sore, but no so confining. I pull in harness, and little brother pushes. I cannot read, and never go to church, as I have no clothes, and mother has nine of us.'

Eight year old Crawford Freedom, who was described as a very delicate little fellow, said:

'Father makes me gang with him in the morning at half-past four, and I return at half-past five. We live in Banton, two miles away. I don't mind the daylight but it is awful dark and a long road after we get in the mine mouth. I am glad to get home, as we have only oatcake and water in the place I work. Been three weeks at work. I was wrought at the school in the big spell and twopenny book.'

James Miller, a 12 year-old coal-hewer, said:

'I worked at picking and riddling coal upwards of two years. I do so as often as the state of the pit will allow. Occasionally much wet in pit, sometimes little bad air. I have fallen asleep often, but has na muckle time to do so now as I am over-sore worked. Before I went down I could read the Bible, but am out of it now. I am trying it again on my idle days.'

Alexander Marshall, a 16 year-old coal-hewer, said:

'I have wrought five years in the Still Mine, and work occasionally on day and night shifts. My usual hours are 12 to 13 daily, for which I get 2s. 6d. on the average of working days, which are eight or nine in the fortnight. The youngest boys working in our pit is nine years of age, many are older but very few read; those who read a little do not write any.'

Robert Rennie, who was just described as a collier, said:

> 'Young boys are used in the narrow seams to draw coal in bogies
> from the wall to the wagon-road. It is very hard work. The
> distance now is 70 to 80 yards. The seams vary from 13 to 24
> inches in thickness. They crawl on their hands and knees. The
> harness they wear is similar to horses, and they draw the bogies
> up and down the braes. My younger brother, Allen Rennie, was
> killed a short time since in this mine by the roof falling while
> he was slyping in a narrow seam. He died momentarily.
> Another died from similar mischance very lately (John
> Forsyth). But these matters are taken no notice of in Scotland,
> even amongst the most responsible classes.'

Hugh Campbell, a ten year-old coal-filler, said:

> 'I have helped to fill father's hutchies for twelve months.
> Sometimes I shove them with brother. If I do not do my
> bidding I get my licks, sometimes the belt and whiles the pick-
> shaft. I go down at five and six in the morning and return at
> five at night.'

Walter Jarvie, manager of Cadell's mine at Banton which supplied
ironstone for the Carron company, said:

> 'There is a vast deal of carbonic acid gas in the mines, arising
> from the metals, which causes the men to drop off early, as it
> creates a kind of asthma. In the small village of Banton there
> are nearly 40 widows, and as the children work always on the
> parents behalf, it prevents them having recourse to the kirk-
> session for relief.'

If conditions were wretched for the children, the elderly also
suffered. Duncan McKinley, a 60 year-old collier said:

> 'I wrought many years at Townhead, and my sons work below

now, and have done from childhood. Wife and I are supported by them. Poor bodies like us after the work is out might as well die, for the kirk-session care nought about us. There are many old couples hereabout who have no bairns near them, that after great begging only get 2s.6d. a month out of the poor's money, and my sons would sooner we should hang upon them than be starved by the parish.' (1)

It was a perfect cycle of exploitation. The men died prematurely through accident or illness, and their children replaced them to face a similar fate.

As the depression of the early 1840s deepened soup kitchens were set up in Kilsyth to stave off starvation, and on the February 11th 1842 a public meeting was held in the Mason's Hall to petition both Houses of Parliament in a call to abolish the Corn Laws, 'which are at the moment grinding the faces of the poor and bringing great numbers of them to a premature grave.'

Bailie Rowatt told the meeting that he had attended meetings on the subject in Glasgow and Edinburgh. 'Never in my life have I heard so many statements of misery and wretchedness from men from all parts of Scotland and England,' he said. They called for a total and immediate repeal of the laws, which, of course, was ignored.

The Kilsyth agitation brought a bizarre response. An article appeared in a Glasgow newspaper claiming that a survey of the condition of the Kilsyth weavers revealed there were no cases of destitution. The weavers were incensed to find that their appalling suffering was not only being ignored, but dishonestly denied. Fourteen signed a letter to the newspaper.

'Would to God it were true that there were no cases of destitution to be found in Kilsyth,' they wrote.

'Alas mournful cases are to be found on every hand. The author of this untrue, immoral and unChristian statement we do not exactly know. We, however, do believe that a factor and two or three of his subalterns were responsible. We pity them as slaves to their Corn Law masters.

'We again repeat that the general averages given of the earnings of the weavers in Kilsyth do not exceed 2/10d per week after deductions for light, loom, rent, carriage, starching, twisting etc... that the average allowance for each dependant upon each loom does not exceed 1/5d and that these are particular cases of four, five and six individuals depending upon the earnings of one loom.

'We aver, and without fear of contradiction, that the great majority of the weavers in Kilsyth are in great poverty and destitution – that they are fast progressing towards a state of pauperism and meanness. Truth must be told, and shall be told, in high quarters, that unless the Corn and Provision Laws are repealed there is but one alternative left to the poor and able tradesman, and that is, he must have bread for himself and family, or – die.' (2)

The dire plight of the weavers was widespread. In a talk in 1838 Thomas Carlyle told of the social unrest he found in the north of England. In one place he heard a loom at work till twelve o'clock at night, and was told a weaver next door, a man with a wife and six children, earned six shillings a week for his seventeen hours of daily work.

'Whether we pay them well or ill, we treat them equally as mere machines,' he wrote. 'In many places they are forming societies for purchasing rifles by a subscription of a penny a week.' He predicted: 'We shall soon have insurrection, and these poor creatures must be put down by the sabre and the gallows, and then perhaps thinking men will be roused to seek for a remedy.'

For Kilsyth, the saviour in the 1800s was coal mining, but, as we have seen, at a horrendous human cost. Coal was to fuel the new industrial order which created the country's wealth, but the real price was paid in the lives and health of the miners. Safety in those days was not a secondary consideration, it was not a consideration at all. It was not only the horrific loss of life in the frequent disasters across the coalfield, which so often wiped out families and decimated whole communities, but the daily injuries and broken health of miners that was so shocking; the contrast of those finely sculptured bodies shaped by hard labour enclosing the lungs of relatively young men which were rotted by poisonous gas and coal dust.

The carnage became so common as to be seen as normal. As late as 1900, Robert Anderson recalls walking down the Backbrae and seeing a small group of people looking towards the Haugh Pit. On inquiry, he was told a man had been killed and they were waiting to see the body brought to the pithead.

Coal mining is the one subject in which Robert Anderson displays deep emotion.

'I have been at bedsides unsurpassed for sadness in the cockpit of a Man of War or the hospitals of a battlefield. I have seen the victims dying with crushed-in ribs, injured spines or mangled thighs. Some I have known who lived, only to go about in crutches all their days, with trailing feet. I hate the mining industry with all my heart, and the necessity that men should win their bread by it. One time, on arrival at a house, I found four of my own church members, a father and three sons, stretched on shake-downs on the kitchen floor. Their poor faces and arms, burned black, were covered by oil-steeped cloths. There were holes for their eyes and nostrils and mouth. It was a ghastly sight, and to me an intolerable price to pay for bread and butter.'

There had been coal mining in and around Kilsyth on a small scale for many years, but in many parts of Scotland there had been a substantial mining industry for centuries. Like the weavers who were to follow them, the story of those early miners was excised from the history books. Can anyone of mature years recall being told at school that as late as 1799, when the weaving industry was well established, Scottish coal miners were still slaves, who were bought and sold as part of the pits in which they were condemned to work for life?

Under an Act of Parliament of 1606, no miner could be employed without a testimonial from his last employer, and a miner who left his work without leave could be reclaimed within a year and a day by his employer. The coal owners, who were normally the landowners, had the legal powers to withhold wages, impose fines, scourge or put miners in the stocks or in prison. In *Sketches of Early Scotch History* Hugh Miller gives a harrowing account of conditions in a slave mining village outside Edinburgh.

> 'The houses were a wretched assemblage of dingy, low-roofed, tile-covered hovels. The collier women, poor over-toiled creatures, carried all the coal up a long turnpike stair, inserted in one of the shafts, and it was calculated that each day's labour was equivalent to carrying a hundredweight from the sea level to the top of Ben Lomond. No wonder, poor things, they cried like children under their load, no wonder a peculiar type of mouth. . . wide, open, thick-lipped, projecting equally above and below. . . like savages was developed, but it is a matter of extreme wonderment that this sort of thing should be going on in Scotland at the very time our sapient legislators were making St Stephen's ring with denunciation of negro slavery.'

Kilsyth had mercifully escaped the excesses of the first phase of Scottish coal mining, but was to become heavily involved in the second coming of the industry. By the 1820s the growth of coal was becoming more noticeable in the streets of the town as the white aprons of the weaver contrasted incongruously with the coal black faces and apparel of the miners. The industry was to grow rapidly and took off spectacularly when William Baird & Company, who were to become the largest employers in Scotland, moved into the Kilsyth district in 1860. The deep coal mining provided more work, profits and tragedies. The environment also changed beyond recognition.

From being a small country town, Kilsyth was transformed into a hive of unregulated heavy industry with noise day and night, grime, fumes and dust along with the indiscriminate coal waste bings which were not removed until midway through the twentieth century by public funding. Kilsyth had been blessed with a number of natural springs supplying quality water throughout the town, but they also fell victim to contamination from underground workings.

If the workplace of those miners and their children were places of back-breaking, soul-destroying and life-threatening danger, there was little material comfort for them when they returned home. In 1875 a survey of miners' houses was carried out over central Scotland. When the reporter visited Kilsyth he did not disguise his revulsion.

'Kilsyth, is without exception, the dirtiest town I have visited, although its situation is such that its rulers might easily reverse this state of things if they wished to do so.' He went on:

> 'In all communities of the same size there are lanes and closes which will not bear inspection, redeemed by others of cleanlier appearance, but Kilsyth is consistently dirtier throughout. Ashpits are erected right under house windows and lie reeking and smelling of accumulated filth, which is not removed with regularity. I was told by some of the tenants it is not taken away at all, but simply laid under ground when the season for delving comes round. Many of the tenements are very old and rickety.'

He concluded: 'This at all events is plain, that Kilsyth is very much in need of a sanitary revival, if not an improvement Act'.

It should be noted that responsibility for these shocking conditions rested with local private landlords, and there was no bigger landlord than the Edmonstones. There are numerous letters still in existence from their lawyers and factors threatening poor people who did not have the money to pay rent and feu duties for the right to live in their hovels.

It is little wonder that the Reporter should write: 'After the squalor of the town it was quite a relief to come to Auchinstarry which lies between Kilsyth and Croy Station'.

There he found three rows of substantial stone-built one-storey houses, and a fourth row under construction. They were built by Baird the coalmasters, and had wooden floors with a tarpaulin underneath and ventilation on both sides of the house to carry a current of air underneath. There were three large outbuildings erected for each row, comprising a wash-house and boiler for every six tenants, coal cellars for all, and closets and ashpits for every three tenants. There was also a caretaker and inspector to manage the rows. The Reporter recalled:

> 'I went into one of the houses in the dusk of evening and found the tea things laid out on a tablecloth of snowy whiteness, with which the general appearance of the kitchen pleasantly corresponded. Here at last, is evidence that if miners get really good dwellings they will take pride in them, and rival their neighbours in home attractions.'

The Baird Company were no philanthropists. They needed miners in the area to work their pits. They charged high rents, and no doubt ensured they profited from the enterprise. They also gained the power of eviction, which gave them another hold over their miners. But at least they provided habitable homes which were properly managed.

As late as 1911 Kilsyth and Armadale in West Lothian were identified as the two worst housed areas in Scotland. Kilsyth came second to Armadale with the highest number of people sharing a room with at least three others, and topped the list with the highest number of single ends.

The new industrial order did bring rewards. It ended the relative isolation of the town with a new canal boat, the Swiftboat, which made the journey from Auchenstarry to Glasgow in one and three quarter hours. Then in 1846 the Glasgow-Edinburgh railway line was opened, with its station at Croy, which widened access to the outside world, followed by two local railway lines in the town of Kilsyth itself. Anderson was perhaps pitching it a bit high when he said Kilsyth had become a suburb of Glasgow, but it probably felt that way at the time.

As we have observed, secular and church politics were intertwined, and to understand one it was helpful to be aware of the other. In those heady days of 1832 another conflict storm began to take shape as the Church of Scotland and the Government locked horns. Again the conflict had nothing to do with doctrine but was about the independence of the Church, and again centred on the issue of patronage – the right of congregations to appoint their minister. The battle raged for a decade and when it became clear the establishment would not release its hold on the Church, came the Great Disruption of 1843.

In the largest and most dramatic split in the Church's history 121 ministers, led by their retiring Moderator, walked out of the General Assembly in Edinburgh and marched down the hill to Tanfield Hall at Canonmills to form the Free Church of Scotland under the leadership of the charismatic Dr. Thomas Chalmers. Amongst that procession was the Rev. William Burns the parish minister of Kilsyth. This reserved, elderly and conventional man was the most surprising rebel. Yet, this was an act of stunning and principled courage by those ministers who surrendered their incomes, manse, glebes and pulpits to secure the freedom of the Church in Scotland.

It was said that the face of Dr. Burns turned deadly pale when he heard his old church bell ringing on the Sabbath morning after his return from Edinburgh, knowing that never again would he mount the pulpit where he had faithfully ministered to his congregation for twenty three years. However, he was backed by almost his whole congregation who bought him a house in Charles Street. The Relief Church provided help and accommodation until a new church and manse was built at the top of Howe Road, and Dr. Burns went on to minister to his people for another sixteen years.

Happily, the story did not end there. Necessary as it was, the cohesion and authority of the Church had been compromised by the secessions, yet, only four years later, in 1847, the work of reunification began when the Relief Church joined up with the other secession churches from the previous century to form the United Presbyterian Church, of which the present UP Lane is a reminder. It was said that William Anderson played an influential role in bringing this first act of union to fruition.

Then in 1900, in a major step forward, the United Presbyterians joined forces with the Free Church of Scotland to form the United Free Church. That same year, the splendid new church was built at Parkfoot, and it was unanimously decided by both congregations in the new united church that it should be named the Anderson United Free Church, in honour of John Anderson and his son Robert whose remarkable joint ministries in Kilsyth extended to one hundred and seven years. Robert Anderson predicted then, that would not be the end of unification though he would not live to see it. He was correct on both accounts.

In 1929 a momentous event took place when the United Free Church rejoined the Church of Scotland – but significantly on the terms laid down by Thomas Gillespie, John Anderson and those other heroic seceders. It had taken 168 years of sacrifice, suffering and struggle but the freedom and integrity of the National Church had been secured.

It is not the purpose of this narrative to explore the complex and torturous history of religion in Scotland but we must guard against the misconception that it can be simply reduced to a clash between a democratically inclined Church of Scotland and a feudal Episcopalian Monarchy.

But what became of the advance of democracy in which the freedom and rights of the people rested, and in which the weavers had contributed so much to advance? In those heady days of 1832 few could have imagined it would take a few years short of a century before Britain could be accurately described as even a semi-democracy. Every small advance was resolutely resisted with the normal weapons of the establishment, repression, corruption, victimisation, imprisonment and loss of life.

Whatever conclusions we arrive at from the weavers' story two appear incontrovertible: the democratic rooted liberties we enjoy today were not granted from above, but won at great cost from below. We will never know all the stories of the countless number of men and women who were victimised, imprisoned, transported or driven beyond Scotland's shores for daring to proclaim the cause of democracy. Secondly, those old Kilsyth weavers not only played a part in lifting this land to a higher plane of civilisation, but played a highly courageous and significant part.

Why then should we rescue their story from the mists of history? The historian and statesman Tom Johnston provides one reason. 'A democracy ignorant of the past is not qualified either to analyse the present or to shape the future,' he said.

The weavers' pastor and contemporary, Robert Anderson, suggested a more personal reason.

'It is difficult to realise the times of our forefathers, who had to suffer and battle for the rights we enjoy,' he said. 'It would be wrong to the memory of heroes who did not fight for fame, and it would be to our loss if sometimes the past was not recalled, and the sense of our obligation revived, to those who nobly bore the stress of trial and transmitted to their children a better than their own inheritance.'

Perhaps as good and all-embracing reason for restoring and cherishing the memory of those old Kilsyth weavers is simply to repay a debt of honour.

(1) Childrens Employment Commission 1842

(2) *Glasgow Chronicle* February 28th 1842

(3) Johnston Thomas *The History of the Working Classes in Scotland*
    Forward Publishing Company

INDEX